Alienation
and Identification

Alienation
and Identification

Morton A. Kaplan

THE FREE PRESS
A Division of Macmillan Publishing Co., Inc.
NEW YORK

Collier Macmillan Publishers
LONDON

The Free Press
A Division of Macmillan Publishing Co., Inc.
866 Third Avenue, New York, N.Y. 10022

Collier Macmillan Canada, Ltd.

Library of Congress Catalog Card Number: 76-8146

Printed in the United States of America

printing number

1 2 3 4 5 6 7 8 9 10

Library of Congress Cataloging in Publication Data

Kaplan, Morton A
    Alienation and identification.

    Includes bibliographical references and index.
    1. Alienation (Philosophy) 2. Identity.
3. Justice. I. Title.
B808.2.K36   170   76-8146
ISBN 0-02-916790-6

Contents

Preface

Alienation and Identification is the second of two closely related books, the first of which is *Justice, Human Nature, and Political Obligation.* My basic position concerning ethics is stated there. The good is objective, but not independent of the purposive subject in actual and potential environments. Ethical rules, therefore, cannot be validated in abstraction from an examination of society, man, and nature. The subject matter of ethics primarily lies in the arena of praxis; and our beliefs about it are based on evidence that, for the most part, lies at the periphery of the field of knowledge, where the structure of the field is relatively weak and where different legitimate interpretations are possible.

There is another body of literature, however, that on the whole is scoffed at by professional philosophers as irrational or anti-intellectual. This is the literature on alienation that recently has been taken over by counterculture or pop culture enthusiasts. I do not disagree about the anti-intellectuality of much, if not all, of this literature, at least in its recent dress. And I reject its conclusions. But it has an honorable history that in modern times can be traced to Hegel and Marx.

Moreover, it recognizes what much of the professional literature in the social sciences does not: the ontological aspect of
justice. Its *cri de coeur* may be misplaced, but it is not
irrelevant. And unless we understand its message, however
ineptly or even mischievously it is stated, our rejection of its
thrust will be ill conceived.

Therefore, I believe, it is useful to examine some of the
claims raised in the contemporary literature on alienation.
However, I shall be especially, although not exclusively, concerned with those aspects of the literature that are related to
its Hegelian and Marxian foundations. In my opinion, this is
the most intellectually respectable segment of the tradition.
And, thus, it can be subjected more easily to rational analysis. In my opinion, the advocates of this position make
mistakes that are often the obverse of those I criticize in
Justice, Human Nature, and Political Obligation. If John
Rawls's and Stephen Toulmin's mistakes on the whole, even
though not exclusively, are mistakes in theorization, the
"theorists" of alienation make mistakes primarily in the
realm of conceptualization and of metatheory—an aspect of
praxis that deals less with specific assessments than with a
more general and discursive account of the constraints on
theorizing. If the "pure" theorists of justice are excessively
abstract and rule-oriented, most theorists of alienation fail to
give appropriate weight to the importance of rules and the
complexity of the interrelationships between individuals and
social institutions. The contemporary emphasis of many
philosophers of ethics upon ethical rules and that of many
theorists of alienation upon authenticity both ignore, or at
least fail to treat adequately, the problem of identification:
the crucial link between the purposive, good-seeking human
system and the body of ethical rules to which it accords
legitimacy. Although this subject is touched upon in chapter
4 of *Justice, Human Nature, and Political Obligation,* it
receives a different treatment in this book: one that I hope
assists in the reader's understanding of it. I realize that this

comment will remain somewhat opaque, however, until the relevant portions of the book clarify it.

This book is divided into two parts: "Metatheory" and "Analysis." Part 1 attempts briefly to explore why the concept of alienation became so important in the great philosophical tradition beginning with Hegel and Marx. Chapter 1 will attempt to show how the importance of the concept emerges from Hegel's attempt to solve the problem of knowledge that Kant had bequeathed: a problem rooted in seventeenth-century mechanism. Marx's attempt to demystify the kernel of the Hegelian dialectic also failed; and its failure produced the "scientific" and "humanistic" variants of his position. I shall examine both and show how they overemphasize some important aspects of Marx's doctrine at the expense of others in an unsuccessful effort to resolve the problems he left unsolved.

Chapters 2 and 3 will attempt to resolve these problems from within the framework of knowledge and inquiry that Marx was attempting to develop. The important distinction between theory and praxis that was emphasized in *Justice, Human Nature, and Political Obligation* will play a significant role in this discussion. Human values will be restored to the universe of science. Some of the most vexing problems in the sociology of knowledge will be resolved. The mystical kernel will be removed from the dialectic, and the coating will go with it. As a result, the concept of alienation will be demystified and reduced to secondary importance—a result consistent with the analysis in part 2.

Because I believe the mistakes of most writers on alienation are primarily conceptual, I shall, for the most part, treat the topics of part 2 on analysis at that level. Because the concepts are used so loosely and inconsistently by these theorists and because they are applied in such a variety of contexts, I shall on the whole ignore their specific usages and develop my own in chapter 4. Otherwise I should have been forced to write a much longer book that would have added little, if anything, of significance to what I say in this one. I believe that brief exploration of the concepts will show how, why, and where the theorists of alienation fall into the errors I attribute to them. My applications of the concepts via partial theory sketches are intended as illustrations rather than as dogmatic assertions, although my brevity of expression at times may give a different impression.

The problem of identification is crucial. And it has been at the crux of many disputes. Freud, for instance, has often been accused of emphasizing the adjustment of man to society regardless of justice or authenticity. Whether or not this is an accurate interpretation of Freud, the criticism that an emphasis on adjustment tends to ignore problems of justice is correct. Even so, it might be defensible in some circumstances: some personalities may be so "crippled" that no alternatives to adjustment exist; and some societies may be in straits so serious that authentic man—as I shall use that term—might find life unbearable under those conditions. Moreover, as the section, in chapter 5, entitled "Dysfunction of 'True' Autonomy" indicates, relative absolutes (representing a first-order synonymity of interests)—a concept that has some similarities to the Freudian superego—are required for a sense of identity.

A failure to identify with a set of moral codes and with those existential relations to the particular persons or groups to whom the moral code applies relevantly tends to produce that state of anomie that characterizes many alienated individuals. Partial identifications may produce anomie with respect to some systems only. Thus, one may be integrated in the social system but alienated from one's family, or integrated in a revolutionary group but alienated from society at large.

The problem from the standpoint of a theory of justice is to establish a connection between personality needs, the social codes required for existential social systems, and a capacity for the critical evaluation of existential codes from the standpoint of a wider framework of justice.

Although *Alienation and Identification* is closely related to *Justice, Human Nature, and Political Obligation,* and although there are references in each book to the other, it is designed to be read independently. Where this would not entirely work, as in discussions of epistemology and equilibrium in chapters 8 and 9 of this book, about twenty manuscript pages from the other book (although not all in the original sequence) have been included. I believe that this will be sufficient for the purposes of this book, although the reader who wishes a more systematic discussion of these topics will have to turn to *Justice, Human Nature, and Political Obligation.*

Acknowledgments

I wish to thank Franco Ferrarotti, Alan Gewirth, Uwe Nerlich, and David Tracy for comments on chapter 1. Tang Tsou made helpful comments on the appendix. Some comments by John Nelson were particularly useful. The services of my secretary, Kersti Thompson, were invaluable in preparing the manuscript of this book.

Alienation
and Identification

Part 1

METATHEORY

Chapter 1

Origins of the Problem

Although the uses of the concept of alienation are extremely diverse, the reasons it is important in philosophical and political theory illuminate the relationship of science to values, to problems of methodology and of social science theory, and, more generally, to the context within which meaningful questions can be raised.

An inquiry into the origins of the problem, as it is understood in the West, would encompass all of Western intellectual history, a task I am not about to undertake. Fortunately, the aspects of that history that are most central to my inquiry have their origins in the seventeenth century with the rise of modern science. Even so, if what I say is not to be disproportionate to my purpose in saying it, the comments I make in many respects will be schematic. Much that is problematic in the interpretation of great works of philosophy will be treated unproblematically and without great attention to nuances. This would be a grave fault if the schematic character of my examination were likely to have great influence upon the conclusions reached; but I believe that this will not be the case. Therefore, with apologies to those whose interest in exegesis is paramount and with a warning that the relationship of the discussion of the theory of knowledge to alienation will become evident only later, let us begin.

Pre-Hegelian Thought

In its political guise, modernity may have begun with Machiavelli. Yet, it was Galileo and his scientific investigations that gave it its greatest impetus. Galileo began his investigations within a framework of assumptions that some have called Platonic. The consequences of his work, and of the torrent of scientific endeavor that followed it, shattered the medieval view of man and of the world. Descartes's mechanistic philosophy—so closely related to the new view of the physical world—produced various offspring: from the French philosophes to Julien de la Mettrie's *L'Homme machine,* from Berkeley's idealism to the realism of Hobbes and Locke, and from the scepticism of Hume to the Kantian *Critique of Pure Reason.*

If the atomists of the ancient world believed that everything was built from atoms, the mechanists of the modern world started with motion. God was conceived of as a master mathematician who, aware of the initial moving state of all objects in the world, could predict their subsequent detailed histories. If simple motions accounted for the phenomena to which Newton's laws applied, laws would eventually be discovered for the complex motions that man found in society. It was therefore no accident that Hobbes's political philosophy was based upon a philosophy of motion. Motions external to the actors produced qualitative subjective events. These subjective events were copies or reflections of a real external world.

John Locke saw the mind as a blank slate upon which impressions from the external world were received. However, his distinction between primary and secondary qualities carried with it the implication that although secondary qualities responded to characteristics of external objects, they did not copy them. The world external to mind—the objective world of space and time—was the world to which the categories of physics applied and which mental images represented or copied. Truth still existed in Locke's world.

However, Bishop Berkeley, who claimed that men know only representations, could find no objective ground for a belief in this external world, or in the existence of other men, except that belief warranted by a just God. Leibniz developed a monadic theory with, if I may use a metaphoric expression, a coordinating switchboard operated by God that assured that all the windowless monads (which is what men were) experienced representations of the same real-world events.

Hume was traveling in a different, but even more sceptical, direction when he "disproved" knowledge of causality by "demonstrating" that representational perceptions were only of sequences and not of causes. (Hume, however, ignored the fact that the existence of a sequence is an inference from experience rather than a fact of experience and that the relationship between sensation and experience is far more complex than his philosophy allowed.)

By this time, the world of science and of common sense was being pulled down to its knees despite the obvious successes of objective, scientific methodology. The discordance between philosophic analysis and scientific power presented a dilemma. In an age in which knowledge was of a kind and scope that was unprecedented in human history, scepticism concerning the foundations of knowledge was rising to its highest point.

Immanuel Kant made the first major effort at reconstruction. His *Critique of Pure Reason,* in which he claimed that Hume had awakened him from his dogmatic slumber, established causality as a necessary category of mind. The categories employed by the mind in coping with the world were *a priori.*

However, just as Hume's theory was subject to the rejoinder that his associational theory of mind was inherently causal—for propinquity and frequency or strength of sensation produced the idea of cause in the mind according to his explanation—Kant's philosophy was subject to the criticism of Trendelenberg, who argued that Kant's obversion of Hume was merely superficial and that the *Ding an sich* was irrelevant to experience in the Kantian system.

Thus Kant's *Critique* failed to satisfy the quest for true knowledge. Causality applied only to representations and not to real things. And his synthetic *a priori*s that gave meaning to representations assumed a world that was counterfactual. Kant assumed that representations occurred in discrete sequences, that the sequences were invariant in a (reified) space/time, and that this permitted an adequate explanation of the concept of cause (and hence of scientific theory or explanation). Furthermore, truth concerned representations only; and even in this form it was lodged in the subjective capacity of the transcendental ego. It did not penetrate to ultimate reality. Or, from a critical perspective, only representations were real in which case the Kantian philosophy collapsed, including its warranty for belief. Thus, by the turn of the century, Kant's philosophy was viewed as unsatisfactory.

Hegel and Marx

Attempts were made to restore content to the idea of truth that included Fichte's unconscious ego—an ego that came to consciousness by "butting" against an external obstacle—and Schelling's naturalism. Fichte's solution to the problem of knowledge represented a return to an interactive framework of reference. In this sense, it helped prepare the way for the Hegelian solution. Alienation as a key philosophic category arises out of the Hegelian solution to the problem of knowledge.

The path can be found in the writings of the young Hegel of the Jena period. Man's image of himself, for example, arises out of his interaction with other men and from his recognition of himself in their image of him.

The Hegelian (and also the Marxian) theory of knowledge assumed that interactions among men and with the natural world produced knowledge. The Hegelian system dispensed with the concept of representation as a copy of an external reality, for appearance was how something was presented to an external observer. Marx may be interpreted in the same fashion, although he does speak of searching for a theory that "mirrors" reality; and it is this aspect of Marx that probably led Lenin to a copy theory of truth. It is possible that the break with the mechanistic conception of knowledge that was introduced by Hegel was so radical that neither man fully understood its implications. Alternatively, it is possible that the Newtonian model of science inherent in the seventeenth-century mechanistic philosophy was still so influential that each accepted elements of it. We have no need to decide these points to reach our conclusions.

The young Hegel, and his seventeenth-century forerunner, Giambattista Vico, placed this interactive process in human history. It was no longer enough to speak of man in general or in the abstract. Instead there are historical men whose characteristics represent the concrete conditions of their time. However, as man enters history, he builds institutions or societies in which essential aspects of him are objectified in the sense that the patterns of activity and intention are perceived as structures. They become alienated from him to the extent that their operations are divorced from his individual control or from any meaningful relationship to his purposes. They are reified to the extent that their particular time/space-bound characteristics are perceived as real and as merely copied by the mind. As man labors upon the world, the surplus of his labor that he trades for other things of value to him and the patterns of conduct that become institutionalized represent objectifications that eventually divorce themselves or alienate themselves from his individual purposes.

The Absolute comes to self-knowledge through its partial representations in nature, society, and man. All represent partial, and therefore alienated, aspects of the Absolute: the totality within which all relations are internal and conflict is absent. (The reader will note that this is a far broader and more philosophical use of "alienation" than the sociological application in the previous paragraph.) These partial representations can be understood because Reason governs the world, although it is accessible to mind only insofar as historic conditions permit. (How relevant this qualification is can be understood only by particular and not by general analyses.) Alienation cannot be overcome within history but only in the Absolute. Nonetheless, individual alienations can be overcome as higher stages of self-consciousness are reached.

In the Hegelian philosophy, history was the realm of the accidental; but nonetheless it was a realm in which necessity worked itself out. Each partial expression of the Absolute such as Man, Nature, and Society proceeded according to its own inner logic. In the process, individual men gained truer views of themselves and of society.

The specifics of events were the specifics of history. History in this sense could not be understood except with reference to its concrete details. On the other hand, the sequences or stages of history were necessary in that they represented the unfolding of Absolute Spirit. Thus, as each partial expression of the World Spirit represented itself in ways that became contradictory, it dialectically overcame its current mode of being and entered a higher stage. Hegel, however, was never able to articulate how necessity influenced accident and vice versa except by reference to God's mind. Therefore, he could give no articulated account of why the actual was necessary.

Is this last criticism unfair because it implicitly identifies theory with the deductive model of modern science whereas

Hegel took a broader view of theory? A discussion of this question involves the distinction that is made between theory and praxis in *Justice, Human Nature, and Political Obligation* and that is presented in shorter form in the next chapter. Briefly, theory is identified with the hypothetico-deductive model, à la Hempel. However, theory is not confirmable in an absolute sense. The interpretation both of the character of evidence and of its validity in particular tests depends upon the realm of praxis. In the realm of praxis the entire field of knowledge—including other theories, propositional and empirical knowledge, and an assessment of their "fitting-ness," consistency, and partial relatedness—determines the assessments that are reached with respect to the theory in question.

If we treat Hegel's philosophical schema as a theory in the hypothetico-deductive sense, it obviously fails, for it then becomes dependent on information not included within it. In this case, the disjunction between theoretical schema and historical outcomes is inevitable.

However, let us suppose that Hegel treats the philosophy of history according to the methods of praxis. In this case, necessity is not a possible attribute of assessment. Necessity is an attribute of logical entailment within the hypothetico-deductive method which treats theorems as if they were known to be laws and as if the parameters of theory and the conditions of application were completely and finally known.

On the other hand, although it may make sense to speak of assessments within praxis as virtually certain on occasion—because of the weight of evidence and because the "fitting together" of various theoretical schemas is so well struc-tured—necessity in the sense of the hypothetico-deductive model is not an applicable concept.

Even more important, the closer we come to the human and social elements of history, the "looser" in general is "fit" and the wider is variability in the use of evidence and the assessment of relationships. Moreover, the closer we come to the human or social, the greater the role of "accidents" or particular events in the determination of outcomes.

The sets of categories used by Hegel (and, later, those used by Marx) are highly general—for example, rule by one, by several, by many; capitalism or socialism. No argument that operates at this high level of generality can account for transitions from one to another state of the world. Hegel is no more able to use his categories to characterize the present as a necessary sequel of the past than to predict the future, for assessments of past transitions always require knowledge of particularities that are always accidental in terms of the level of generalization he employed.

On the other hand, we will soon see that Marx's particular examinations of historical transitions, even if counterfactually they were fully adequate, cannot bear the weight of the generalizations he derives from them, for instance, the transition to socialism. His generalizations are disjoined from the particularities of the patterns of his historical explanations. He has not attempted to assess the range of conditions under which particular transitions will occur and those under which they will not. He has not articulated the relationships of relevant historical particularities to the "march" of his higher level categories. And he has allowed variance in that "march" only with respect to unimportant nuances or possible, if unlikely, exceptions.

However, before we consider Marx's philosophical response to Hegel's system, it is necessary to say a few words about other contemporary responses to the intellectual ferment that characterized German thought during the breakdown of the vast intellectual synthesis that Hegel had produced. Sören Kierkegaard, who had sat in on Hegel's lectures on the philosophy of history, and who felt imprisoned by its iron logic, emphasized those aspects of the system that centered on the illumination of human minds as they interacted with others and the material environment. Alternatively, historicist derivations from Hegel—and their positivist counterparts—looked to the "objective" conditions of the material world in their manifold aspects. In the historicist case, culture and society were investigated in their collective aspects with respect to their particular history and characteristics. However, as the historicists investigated history rather than History, and in the absence of World Spirit, each society was *sui generis,* and its values were valid only for it. Thus, the breakdown of Hegelian doctrine produced two contrasting and derivative alternatives. Existentialism, which is a diffuse philosophic movement, in many of its manifestations sought for meaning and identity in self-revelation through intercourse with other selves. Truth rested on faith that might be absolute in its claims, or, as with Kierkegaard, even irrational in its premises. Such faith was subjective and relative to the holder's psyche. Historicism found truth in objective culture and society, but its truth was relative to the uniqueness of the source. Whereas Hegel's system was designed to synthesize the external and the internal, its derivatives were oriented toward one or the other. As we shall soon see, the problems arising from the Marxian system gave rise to similar antithetical derivatives, which we shall examine via Althuser and Habermas. This antithetical dualism is indeed one of the central contemporary philosophical problems.

Before we attempt to cope with the philosophical problem, however, we must recognize that the antithetical derivatives of Hegelian theory called into question the category of alienation. Although alienation might become theological, in the sense of man's being alienated from his faith, or cultural, in the sense of his becoming alienated from a specific culture, the intellectual synthesis on the basis of which alienation had been given a specific and important philosophical meaning had broken down.

Marx attempted to avoid such a dichotomous response. He was satisfied with neither a certainty that was based on faith nor a historical positivism that prevented a critique of existing institutions. Thus, although I am gravely oversimplifying, Marx rejected these alternatives and attempted to find an alternative method for avoiding the metaphysical elements of the Hegelian system in a manner that would be consistent with human freedom. Nevertheless, Marx's effort in its own way was as "totalistic" as Hegel's.

The grand synthesis had already collapsed, however, and this left Marx with a problem concerning truth. If all existing beliefs were partly in error, how could one distinguish between truth and error? If all existence was merely a manifestation of Idea, truth lying only in the totality of the Absolute, which aspects of which beliefs constituted truth and which falsity? Given the cunning of History, how could one know what was its end? Although Hegel had said explicitly that the owls of Minerva take wing only when night falls, others interpret him as having said that philosophy died with him and that the Prussian state represented the Absolute on earth, within which the philosopher could find absolute truth. If this latter conclusion were accurate, again there would be no way of justifying it within the framework of current philosophy. Marx had to find some other standpoint from which truth could be found.

Marx called the methodology he developed historical materialism. It is not necessary to explicate this doctrine in detail, although it is useful to indicate its general outlines and its relationship to the concept of alienation.

Marx started with the concept of natural labor. If knowledge is acquired through the labor man performs, that is, through his interaction with other men in the use of natural resources, then the concept of labor assumes a primary function in philosophy. It becomes the foundation not merely of economic theory but of sociological theory and of the theory of knowledge as well. To speak of labor, Marx decided, requires an analysis of both the forces and the relations of production.

This became the basis of the dialectic that produces the movement of history on earth. Because knowledge is acquired through human interaction, these interactions—again I am greatly oversimplifying—create interests that men are disposed to protect. In societies in which men exploit other men—that is, in which one man's labor is expropriated by another—they will have an interest in distorting the character of the exploitation. This produces ideology, illusion, and error.

These key concepts are used by Marx to make concrete historical analyses that attempt to demonstrate the existence of exploitation in particular societies. The specific forms that this exploitation takes stem from the specific historical circumstances that produced them. The same methodology is designed to explain how true knowledge can be achieved: namely, a society in which domination and, therefore, exploitation no longer exist is one in which there is no interest in, and hence no production of, ideology. Moreover, because man is no longer exploited, alienation also is absent. Therefore, the key to the analysis is in the categories of the relations and the forces of production. This is the central focus of Marx's class analysis. For the same reason, it provides the justification for the belief that in the classless society truth will be possible and exploitation and alienation non-existent.

An allied aspect of this analysis is that in class societies in which domination therefore exists, ideology is necessary, for the ruling class cannot rule without it. Therefore, bourgeois formal equality and bourgeois humanism are merely distortions of these concepts because they are merely formal. They are historically valuable, as Marx attempts to demonstrate; but they cannot eliminate alienation.

A number of problems plague Marx's solutions. The concept of surplus value cannot be related to empirical or theoretical economic analysis. According to the Marxian "law" of value the exchange value of an object is equal to the average amount of socially necessary labor required to create it. It is easy to see why Marx added the qualifier "socially necessary" to his labor theory of value. Had he not done so, he would have been unable to explain why labor expended on objects that people did not want failed to produce exchange value. On the other hand, the qualifier is either incorrect or the "law" is mistakenly formulated.

If "socially necessary" refers to the production of what people really need—assuming that we have some method for determining real needs—exchange value and "real" value would not be identical except by coincidence. Therefore, it would not be possible to relate Marx's concept of surplus value to a theory of capitalism. If, on the other hand, one identifies exchange value with what people actually want, as these wants are expressed in a given system of production and distribution, the "law" is defectively stated.

In the latter case, one needs to ask what is necessary to produce a good at that exchange value: and this depends upon the entire system of what the Marxian school calls the forces and relations of production. The quality and quantity of labor—which Marx obscures under his concept of "average"—management, scarcity, scale of activity, profit and interest as modes for allocating scarce resources, and entrepreneurial skill are among the necessary variables in the production of a good at its exchange value, albeit with some inexactitude and ambiguities in measurement. A similar critique applies on the demand side. And, with recognition of this, the utility for theory of Marx's concept of surplus value collapses.

Thus, socialism and Communism, whatever other arguments might be made for them in terms of different theoretical analyses, are fetishes as Marx deals with them. Moreover, the distinctions between the stages of socialism and Communism—socialism is a system in which each produces and receives according to his abilities and Communism is one in which each produces according to his abilities and receives according to his needs—are are abstract concepts of the kind that Marx argued against when he denounced bourgeois conceptions of man.

Abilities and needs do not exist as universal abstractions that are divorced from the concrete conditions of life. Because Marx believed that capitalism provided workers with only the minimum requirements for human reproduction—which was not true even in the Europe in which he wrote, as the Asian laborer would have been well aware—he overlooked the fact that society must provide those rewards, whether economic or of some other type, that encourage individuals to acquire the skills and engage in the activities that are needed to maintain or develop their society, including provision for the needs of others. These needs may differ from society to society, again depending upon the characteristics of individuals, their individual experiences, and the degree of their self-knowledge.

Moreover, a philosopher of values might argue that people need whatever is required to make each one the best kind of person that lies within his individual potentiality. Although it is possible to conceive of a type of man and of a social system in which the most desirable forms of distribution would be equal, this is highly unlikely in complex systems and perhaps unlikely in view of the diverse characteristics of human nature.

None of the foregoing implies that the distributions entailed by the market in a capitalist society are best or that optimal societies would permit the wrecking of lives that occurs in every known society including the United States, Russia, and China. However, it is clear that the fetishistic use of the concept of value in Marxian theory renders inadequate the justification of the argument that Communism will eliminate alienation.

It is ironical that interpretations may be placed on Marx's definition of Communism that justify capitalistic distribution. Some economists argue that the market, except where it is prevented by monopoly, provides only those marginal rewards required to elicit "socially necessary" productive (or artistic) skills—that is, those skills required to satisfy the needs of others to the extent possible within a given level of production.

Such an argument assumes a model that overlooks the kinds of choices that a pure market economy forecloses. Moreover, the model is static, whereas the actual economic system is dynamic and subject to environmentally induced disturbances so great that the conclusions of the model do not necessarily apply to concrete individuals or societies. However, the argument is no worse than the sloganeering of contemporary Marxian theory. And it has one justification that contemporary Marxian theory does not have. Marx at least was aware of reification, abstraction, and fetishism. If his thought remained somewhat tainted by the metaphysical abstractions of the then-bourgeois society, current Marxian dogmas, whether of the Russian, Chinese, or Western European variety, forsake the spirit of Marx's inquiries for the particulars of his conclusions.

However, there is an even more basic problem with Marxian analysis. If truth is possible only in a regime without domination and exploitation, how can Marxian theory acquire the mantle of truth if it is developed in bourgeois society and by a bourgeois Karl Marx?

Other questions plague the Marxian analysis of alienation. In Marxian theory, alienation arises because the capitalist takes from the worker his surplus value; that is, the capitalist exploits the worker. Now, it was one thing for Hegel to argue that alienation occurred because the partial manifestations of the Absolute in nature, in institutions, and in man alienated essential elements of a whole from each other. It is quite another thing to argue that a person is alienated because he does not receive all the income from the sale of what he produces, even if we could give a better argument than Marx does for the contention that the capitalist is stealing from the worker or exploiting him. (After all, are not organization and merchandising, as well as capital, part of what produces the product?)

Nor can we argue that if the worker became aware of this "exploitation" he would be alienated because his sense of justice would be offended. This might or might not be true, but it does not follow from the prior arguments. If the argument is that the worker becomes subject to the operations of a system over which he has little or no control and in terms of which he is treated as an object, as Marx sometimes does argue, there is no valid argument in Marx that shows that this is a product of capitalism rather than of complex organization or that complex organization can be avoided under socialism. If the latter is not the case, socialization of the means of production would not solve this form of alienation.

Marx at times, particularly in his early period, does carry over from Hegel a concept of a future totality in which alienation and conflict are absent. But Marx's analysis is insufficient to his conclusions and easily can become mystical. Marx does refer to primitive communist societies as harmonious. Certainly traditional societies based on status change more slowly than modern societies. Thus, their conflicts rarely go to the form of the system. However, as we shall see in part 2, such societies also have alienating characteristics. Although Marx does attempt to cap his argument by his reference to the classless character of Communism, we shall show during our analysis of Althuser, and for reasons given in the prior paragraph, that this is unjustified. As a consequence, Marx's concept of alienation is insecurely linked to his "materialistic" analysis.

A similar difficulty attends Marx's reconciliation of contingency and necessity. Although Hegel, contrary to many popular interpretations, recognized history as the realm of accident, he was never able to articulate the relationship between the March of the Idea on Earth, which is necessary in his system, with the accidents that characterize specific events. It is assumed that the two fit together, but the detailed argumentation that would show this is not produced. Marx, who was unsatisfied with this, and who tried to demystify the Hegelian dialectic, reintroduced it through the back door. History is the product of concrete or material occurrences in the real world. However, even though he seemed to recognize that his theories were subject to revision on the basis of evidence, the mature Marx never seriously considered whether reevaluation of his basic categories of materialistic analysis—forces and relations of production, his definition of class, or his categories of social and economic systems—would produce a more adequate system of analysis. Every rearrangement of theory was designed to support his earlier conclusions and set of categories. Only the specifics of his explanations were altered or the Asian case distinguished from the European in terms of the particularities of sequence toward a set, if not precisely inevitable, ending.

Thus, Marx's materialistic dialectic, rather than demystifying the world, remystifies it. Marx perceived how specific analyses of his could be revised on the basis of evidence; but he did not conceive of the possibility that the adoption of altered categories of analysis and the discovery of new evidence might produce a fundamental alteration in the analysis of the sequences of history.

Moreover, there is no consistent articulated relationship that links the dialectics of class movement with Marx's concrete and multidetermined analyses of particular societies. Their relationship is as ghostly as in the case of the Hegelian dialectic in which the Absolute moves toward its predetermined end despite the accidents of history. It is this basic problem, as we shall see, that produces the scientific and "subjective" variants of Marxism, as its practitioners attempt to account for the discrepancies between Marx's theory of how capitalistic development would produce socialism and the post-Marxian history of economic development.

This problem, with variations from time to time, also becomes manifest in Marx's ontology. Although we discuss ·this in very simplified form, it is legitimate to assert that one aspect of the world—nature and the forces of production—is real or material in Marx's view. The rest is culture or superstructure and (essentially) derived from man's conscious interaction with material reality. In this aspect of his thought, Marx seems to be a dualist with a copy theory of knowledge concerning the material. Consciousness is epiphenomenal; knowledge is sensate; and man's mind either falsely or truly re-presents a singular material reality. Although in his thesis on Feuerbach, the young Marx was breaking out of this dualism toward an interactive approach to knowledge and a non-dualist philosophy, the obscurity of his formulations still leads his latter-day followers toward either mechanism or subjectivism.

Although we shall not examine variants of each position other than those of Althuser and Habermas, the method of analysis we use can be applied easily by the reader to those Marxian analysts, such as Marcuse or Adorno, whom we do not analyze.

The failure of Marx to articulate the relationships between his categories of analysis, the conclusions to which they led him, and his concrete analysis remystified the concept of alienation. We shall see that the attempts to overcome this failure also failed. However, before we pursue the failure of the contemporary "scientific" and "humanistic" derivations of Marxian theory—and the consequences of that failure for a theory of alienation—we shall turn to the position taken by an intermediary figure, the father of the modern sociology of knowledge, Karl Mannheim.

Mannheim

Mannheim was dissatisfied with the Marxian concept of ideology. Because he perceived the disjunction between the general analysis of Marx and his specific or more concrete analyses, Mannheim saw no reason why the proletariat as a class should perceive truth. Moreover, Marxian history since the period in which Marx and Engels had written demonstrated convincingly that Marxian doctrine was a doctrine of the intellectuals and not of the workers. Indeed, to the extent that workers supported Marxian parties for doctrinal reasons, they did so because of the slogans that characterized vulgar Marxian doctrine rather than because of the more sophisticated analyses of Karl Marx or of his more talented followers.

Therefore, although I am again presenting a position schematically, Mannheim dispensed with the notion that the class interest of the proletariat could be equated with truth. Instead, Mannheim distinguished between ideologies that justified the way things had been and utopias that were plans for the reconstruction of society. Both, however, developed situationally out of the concrete circumstances, interests, and needs of those who responded to them. Because this formulation left a distinct gap with respect to the character of truth, Mannheim assigned a related function to the detached intellectual, the bourgeois who had left his class and who historically had led each advancing class to its successes.

It is easy to see that Mannheim's solution produced more questions than answers. If the viewpoint of each class was biased, then what was the truth in terms of which it was biased? And how would a detached intellectual find it? If the concept of truth was to be dispensed with, then what rational meeting ground was available to produce a dialogue between conflicting classes? If such a dialogue was concerned not with truth but with competing interests, then how could these competing interests be expressed truthfully and objectively? If we were left only with competing interests, then why should the intellectual detach himself from his own class and reattach himself to some other class except in terms of his own interests? Why should he favor the proletariat over the bourgeoisie or over the rich?

One might answer the last question, although Mannheim did not, by arguing that the intellectual detached himself from all classes by choosing his occupation and that he could find a function in society only by serving as a mediator for its conflicting classes: classes that, in the absence of an ability on the part of one to overcome the other, needed to reach some compromise and that would be able to use the intellectuals either as some kind of neutral arbiter or as skilled tacticians in the search for power and income. Yet, in addition to the psychological problem that intellectuals might not like to think of themselves as eunuchs in the service of a vizier, this formulation leaves us with an intellectual problem. Even this last formulation asserts itself as a truthful or objective statement about reality; and, yet, in Mannheim's terms, it is either ideological or utopian.

Mannheim had dispensed with the metaphysical cores of both the Hegelian system and its Marxian offspring. He was left with a shallow relativistic positivism that dispensed with the pretension to a scientific understanding both of human events and of an evaluational understanding rooted in the rise to self-consciousness of humans in interaction with others.

Most of the seminal thinkers who were concerned with the problem of alienation as it arose in the Hegelian and Marxian systems, therefore, were led to an abandonment of the Marxian synthesis for a further development of either, but not both, of its two root characteristics: the "scientific" or the "humanistic." We cannot begin to explore the manifold variations of these attempts, but the reader will be able to see for himself, if he examines other cases, that they tend to fall into the classification we have made and that some variant of the defect we note will be found in each of the positions.

"Scientific" Marxism: Louis Althuser

I choose as the paradigmatic case for the discussion of the "scientific" approach to Marxian thought, Louis Althuser, the French Communist writer. By science, Althuser means objective, universal, and ahistorical theories and covering laws. In the next two chapters, we shall see why this is a fundamental misapprehension of the scientific problem in the social sciences.

Because Althuser chooses a "scientific" solution to his problem, he distinguishes as sharply as he can between the early Marx, who was emerging from the Hegelian and Feuerbachian tradition, and the later, or scientific, Marx. Because this is so, he also wishes to divest Marx of those concepts, such as "totality," that are irrelevant to his use of "science." Thus, he says, the concept of an ideological totality, although valid descriptively, is theoretically invalid, for it exposes the user to the danger of thinking of an empty unity of a described whole rather than of a "determinate unitary structure."[1] Indeed, Althuser believes that an intellectual approach that uses such vague and abstract concepts as "totality" produces a form of alienation. The German intellectual movement of the 1830s and the 1840s, the world in which the Hegelian system was breaking down, he says, produced an ideology that was mystifying and that alienated intellectuals from the "real problems and real objects which were *reflected* in it."[2] Apart from the fact that Althuser's use of the term "reflect" or "reflection," unless it is merely careless—and it does not seem to be careless—represents a return to the copy theory of knowledge, his statement has much to commend it. However, as we shall see, he is unable to develop this insight. In the meantime, it is necessary to follow his argument a bit further.

Althuser argues that history is overdetermined. One meaning of "overdetermination" is that more influences produce an event than are necessary to explain it. Althuser's use of the term, however, is not made explicit and is elucidated only by example. In his discussion, Althuser attempts to give meaning to his use by sharply distinguishing the Marxian dialectic from the Hegelian. He argues that the Marxian dialectic can be explained only in terms of concrete circumstances rather than in terms of abstract generalizations. Thus, although Marx argued that socialism would develop within the womb of capitalism as the contradictions in the system socialized industry in the most advanced capitalistic state, the concept of the weakest link as used by Lenin explains the Russian Revolution. Because capitalism produced the First World War, humanity entered into an *"objectively revolutionary* situation."[3] The concentration of industry had increased the exploitation of the workers and of economies. The competition between the monopolies made war inevitable and dragged vast masses into it. Therefore the greatest effects of the forces unleashed by capitalism were felt in Russia; and they turned Russia into the weakest link because of *"the accumulation and exacerbation of all the historical contradictions then possible in a single State."*[4] Thus, Russia was the weakest link because it had accumulated as many historical contradictions as was then possible; and it was therefore "at the same time *the most backward and the most advanced nation,* a gigantic contradiction which its dividing ruling classes could neither avoid nor solve."[5]

The reader will immediately see that Althuser has not related any of his concrete historical "overdeterminations" systematically to theories or propositions and that, therefore, they do not serve as evidence for any theory or proposition as he uses those terms. Moreover, he has "saved" the Marxian formulation by redefining "advanced." Marx meant "advanced" in the sense of capitalistic development. Althuser uses "advanced" in the sense of most ready for revolution—a definitional equation rather than a proposition.

Althuser attempts to use the Marxian concept of contradiction and his own concept of overdetermination to save Marxian theory as a scientific theory. They are welded into his basic framework of analysis by the use of categories such as the forces of production, the relations of production, the concept of social class, and the essence of the state. However, Althuser argues that these terms or concepts are to be used determinately. Marx, he says, has given only the "two ends of the chain";[6] it still remains to find out what goes on between the two ends of the chain: on the one hand, *"the determination in the last instance by the (economic) mode of production;* on the other, *the relative autonomy of the superstructures and their specific effectivity."*[7]

Unfortunately, where does this leave us? Because history is no longer inevitable, no failure of a Marxian prediction will invalidate this so-called scientific theory. If a prediction occurs, but in a form different from that predicted, this is explained by "overdetermination." Thus, the revolution occurs in Russia because the system is weakest. If, on the other hand, Kerensky had been able to distribute the land and make peace, the revolution would not have occurred. Therefore, Russia, by definition, would not have been the weakest link and the theory also would have been satisfied.

Now, it is quite true that every scientific theory is of an "if/then" type. The statement that a particular missile system, if fired, will escape earth's gravitational pull will be falsified if the fuel is contaminated or if the launcher is misprogramed. And, although these physical counter-conditions are quite obvious in a manner that is often not possible for the formulations of social science, Marxian theory does not attempt, even semisystematically, to specify the conditions under which it does or does not hold.

Moreover, Althuser's chosen example—the First World War—is subject to the gravest questions, for almost all outstanding trade issues had been settled by 1913; and thus the so-called capitalistic contradictions hardly figure in any reasonable explanation of the First World War, although the problems of the Austro-Hungarian empire and the European mobilization systems do play prominent roles in many explanations. Thus, Althuser makes Marxian theory a determinate theory by making it truistic; for example, the socialist revolution will occur if and when conditions are ripe for it. And even its truisms depend on counterfactual assertions in his illustrative examples.

Worse than the above, there is no articulated relationship between his concepts and their applications under different circumstances. Moreover, if we agree that the determinate meaning of terms such as forces of production, the relations of production, and class can vary from situation to situation, no Marxian theorist has presented—or can present, for reasons we shall give—an articulated argument that shows that these variations will be consistent with the conclusions of Marxian analysis. According to the Marxian argument, social relationship to the forces of production determines class. If all own the forces of production jointly, all belong to the same class and have an identity of interests. However, this conclusion depends upon the adequacy of the Marxian definition of class and of its use in Marxian propositions concerning social relations and identity of interests. In Marxian analysis interests are exhausted by class relationships; and class relationships are the only important social relations relevant to economic forces and political control. These conclusions cannot be reached by fiat. The only good test is whether they accord with evidence.

Although relationship to ownership clearly does determine some social relations and although these clearly are related to some conflicts—and also to some coincidences—of interest, the conclusion that no other important social differentiations exist, or that possible conflicts of interests are exhausted by the Marxian categories, has surely not been proved, nor even shown to be plausible, by Marxian analysts.

Milovan Djilas claims that the elite in a Communist state constitutes a new class. Certainly their social relationship to production is different from that of ordinary workers. Just as certainly there are existential conflicts of interest between the well-being of ordinary workers and that of the leaders of the state apparatus. Problems of divisions of production, expenditure of time, and distributions of prestige and authority are involved. Some, by virtue of their location in the system, have more authority over these outcomes than do others. Even socialist industries take a "surplus," as Marxians use that concept, from individual workers. That this is not exploitation is arbitrarily definitional: as there is only one class, the surplus remains within the class—a reification that leaves actual people entirely out of account. Yet, if we reject this obvious reification, we are left with all the old questions of alienation and "contradiction." And if we accept it, we are forced to conclude that Communism overcomes the alienation of classes but not of people. Either alternative seems less than adequate to our knowledge of the social and political relationships of individuals within alternative economic systems.

My remarks concerning the alienation of classes were intended as an ironic inference rather than as a serious attribution to Althuser. I have since learned that the current Chinese view of alienation *is* a class-oriented view in which only class needs and not individual needs are pertinent.[8] The Chinese claim that only classes have needs is clearly counterfactual. It is clearly non-Marxian inasmuch as it leaves individuals and their needs out of account. And it fails to cope with problems arising from the character of organized human activities in either socialist or capitalist societies; for general classes—as opposed to organizations—have no existence except as attributes of individuals considered independently. The Marxian class attributes have social existence only in organizations involving the relations of particular individuals with other individuals with respect to the means of production, that is, in particular industrial organizations. Unlike organizations, neither the proletariat nor the capitalist class exists as anything other than an attribute of particular individuals.

In its general form, a Marxian class category is merely an attribute of particular individuals. The concept of needs and hence of alienation is not relevant to such qualitative attributes. In its existential aspects, that is, in the form of a social relation within an organization, we can speak of needs as applying to elements of the relationship, that is, we can speak of the needs of management or of the workers. But in this form, the class categories do not exhaust the existential aspects of the situation and, hence, of needs or alienation.

Thus, even if the Marxian scheme of classification were satisfactory—and I have argued that it is not—the Chinese inference from it concerning alienation would be illegitimate. However, let us return to our critique of Althuser.

Althuser's attempt to develop a scientific Marxian theory, despite all his efforts, retains a mystical core. Despite all his talk of overdetermination and concrete analysis, there are no articulated relationships between concepts, generalizations, and conditions of life. Instead, his propositions are fitted into a series of foreordained conclusions that are left freely floating in some metaspace of the abstract. In short, rather than starting with a set of generalizations and independently measuring a set of initial conditions—as a scientific theory in principle would—Althuser starts with his conclusions and searches for that set of concrete formulations that would seem to be consistent with the conclusions. This is a form not of science but of theology.

Althuser falls into this mechanistic trap by identifying theory (correctly) with the hypothetical deductive aspects of science. However, he fails to recognize that theory, and the explanatory framework provided by it, applies directly only to a selected set of variables and only indirectly to the concrete world of history: that its application is dependent upon theoretically defined terms and boundary conditions, not all of which can be brought within the framework of the theory.

Marx implicitly recognized this problem and attempted to solve it with the concept of dialectics. However, as we shall see in the next chapter, this is the realm of praxis, where assessment plays a major role. There are no laws in this realm, for laws imply the hypothetico-deductive methodology. In assessments in the realm of praxis, formulations accepted tentatively as laws within particular theoretical frameworks may set constraints on the assessment of real-world outcomes; but, as in the use of physics in designing airplanes or building bridges, they do not determine them.

Thus, for instance, it was possible, if not easy, to make an assessment that a Communist revolution was likely in Russia if one took into account the relatively undeveloped state of the economy, the consequences of the war, the failure of the czarist system, the limitations of Menshevik politics, and the organization and leadership of the Bolsheviks. Whether this or another outcome would be likely is roughly similar circumstances in other, less developed nations would depend upon assessments of all these and still other conditions.

Similarly, one might assess economic problems of scale, the feedback of cyclical economic disturbances into the political system, the tendency to assure short-term requirements by oligopolistic practices both on the part of management and labor, and so forth, and predict on the basis of the assessment of these factors evolutionary tendencies in advanced market system economies and the political systems within which they operate. However, whether these constraints would produce socialism—even assuming we could specify precisely what we mean by the term—and a dictatorship of the proletariat, or one of a variety of other alternatives cannot be determined by a theoretical prediction.

This accounts for the gap between Marx's general statements and his concrete historical analyses. The Marxian use of language retains mystical elements. It is not fully liberated in its treatment of language as a tool, and therefore it retains elements of a subject/object dichotomy with its allied copy theory of knowledge. Nor does Marx adequately distinguish between theory and praxis. Rather than refining the methodology that Marx was attempting to develop, however, Althuser reverts to an earlier scientific mechanism.

Because Althuser emphasizes science as theory, Marxian theory in his hands becomes the tool of an elite—although I recognize that I am oversimplifying Althuser's position on this point. Therefore, Althuser is able to justify, although he does not like, the slogans necessary to mobilize the masses to action and the leadership of the proletarian party in bringing about revolution even against resistance by the masses. Although he talks of socialist humanism, this is possible only when socialism has been achieved. Bourgeois humanism is idealistic and abstract, a "negative function of the concept of reality."[9] Without attempting to saddle Althuser with the excesses of Communist regimes, this is clearly the instrument by means of which they can be justified and the source of the objections by humanistic Marxians to Althuser's "scientific" Marxism. Man is dehumanized by an abstract ideology that strips away all his particular features; and his resistance to the ideology is denigrated in service to an abstract commitment to an abstract socialist humanism and an abstract end to alienation.

If this is not quite the cold and hostile universe of the existentialist biologists, such as Jacques Monod, Althuser's world is clearly hostile to the hopes of real men in real societies. His view of science denies the possibility of voluntarism—that social structures can be influenced by human hopes or conceptions. If socialism is not inevitable, no viable alternative is possible. Thus, no boundaries are placed on the justifications that can be offered for the controls placed on human beings. It is easy to see, therefore, why the "humanistic" Marxians so passionately reject his position.

"Humanistic" Marxism: Jürgen Habermas

Perhaps the foremost exponent of what I choose to call "subjective" (or "humanistic") Marxian doctrine is Jürgen Habermas. Of all the humanistic Marxians, Habermas is the most intelligently disciplined, the most responsive to modern social science, and the most disposed to state his theses in a manner that permits public discourse. In common with others among the humanistic Marxians Habermas insists on the unity of the young and the old Marx. This means, in contradistinction to the positive taken by Althuser, that

Habermas places great weight on the self-reflexive aspects of man's coming to self-consciousness as expressed in both the early Marx and the early Hegel.

Habermas waxes indignant at the authority systems in states such as the Soviet Union. He claims that their only possible virtue is in speeding up the process of development. (In any event, most non-Marxians would regard this as a doubtful proposition on the basis of historical experience.) At best, Habermas says, this is an incentive to underdeveloped areas. In advanced capitalist countries, he states, the standard of living has risen so much that among broad strata of the population, "the interest in the emancipation of society can no longer be articulated directly in economic terms."[10] Therefore, he says, alienation in the form of misery is not the significant problem. The real form of poverty is reflected in alienated leisure: "Scurvy and rickets are preserved today in the form of psychosomatic disturbances, hunger and drudgery in the wasteland of externally manipulated motivation, in the satisfaction of needs which no longer are 'one's own end.' "[11] In this sense, Habermas says that the proletariat has been dissolved, although the entire population is proletarian in the sense of lacking control over the means of production. He denies that people's capitalism can cope with this but also denies that the current practices of the Communist states serve as viable examples.

Habermas, drawing upon Marx but also upon modern science and ordinary language philosophy, attempts to unite theory and praxis. Historical materialism, he says, "can be understood as a theory of society conceived with a practical intent, which avoids the complementary weaknesses both of traditional politics and of modern social philosophy; it thus unites the claim to a scientific character with a theoretical structure referring to practice."[12] Habermas admits that Marxian theory today is not satisfactory for advanced capitalism and that he has not treated epistemological questions systematically. However, he argues that his explanatory treatments have made his program for a theory of science clearly discernible, "a theory which is intended to be capable of grasping systematically the constitutive conditions of science and those of its application."[13] He says that he has let himself be guided by the problem posed "by the system of primitive terms (or the 'transcendental framework') within which we organize our experience *a priori* and prior to all science, and do so in such a manner that, of course, the formation of the scientific object domains is also prejudiced by this."[14] In the sphere of instrumental action, he says, objects are encountered of the moving type where things, events, and conditions are experienced that in principle are capable of being manipulated. On the other hand, in inter-actions, of a possible intersubjective communicative type, objects are encountered of the types of speaking or acting subjects that in principle can be understood symbolically. These two object domains—of the empirical-analytic and of the hermeneutic sciences—are based on their respective objec-tifications of reality. Investigations under them are under-taken from the viewpoint either of technical control or of intersubjective communication. He advocates the method-ological comparison of theoretical concepts, logical construc-tion of theorems, the relationship of theory to object-domain, crtieria verification, testing procedures, and so forth. Whereas empirical knowledge can assume the form of causal explanations or conditional predictions, all of which refer to observed phenomena, hermeneutic knowledge, he says, has the form of interpretation of traditional complexes of meaning. Thus, he says, there is a systematic relationship between the logical structure of a science and "the pragmatic structure of the possible applications of the information generated within its framework."[15] The latter is the realm of praxis.

Moreover, Habermas says, the technical and practical in-terests of knowledge are not irrelevant disturbances of cogni-tion but are the determinants of the aspect under which reality is to be objectified and made accessible to experience to begin with. "They are the conditions which are necessary in order that subjects capable of speech and action may have experience which can lay claim to objectivity."[16]

Habermas continues to expand upon the dichotomy between science and hermeneutics. The paradigm of science, he says, is the observation, but of hermeneutics, the dialogue. There is in hermeneutics "no corresponding system of basic measuring operations with which we can coordinate, in an analogous manner, the understanding of meanings based on the observation of signs, as well as a language expressive of a person, that is, in which the understood utterances could be expressed descriptively."[17]

Therefore, a theory of ordinary language communication is required that explains communicative competence in order to permit a controlled translation of tha experience into data. Practical questions are posed with a view to the acceptance or rejection of norms, as opposed to technical questions that are directed to rationally goal-directed organization and instrumental alternatives, once the goals are given. Theories that can serve the purpose of clarifying practical questions are designed to enter into this kind of communicative or self-reflexive hermeneutic praxis. In this area, language communication serves the purpose of reaching an understanding that is confirmed "in a reasonable consensus";[18] otherwise, it does not represent a " 'real' understanding." Although any consensus can be deceptive, Habermas says, the very concept of a deceptive consensus implies that of a rational consensus. Therefore, the concept of a rational consensus is normative and everyone who speaks a natural language "has intuitive knowledge of it and therefore is confident of being able, in principle, to distinguish a true consensus from a false one."[19] This knowledge is called *"a priori"* or "innate."[20] Thus all language games are based on underlying consensuses. And each consensus has at least four claims to validity: the understandability of the utterance, "the truth of its propositional

component, the appropriateness of its performatory com-
ponent, and the authenticity of the speaking subject."[21]
These claims can only be proven in discourse, according to
Habermas.

Habermas caps his discussion of theory and praxis by
distinguishing three functions that, he says, are measured in
terms of different criteria. The first is the formation and
extension of critical theorems, the ordinary subject matter of
science. The second refers to the processes of enlightenment:
in this process, the theorems are applied or tested by the
initiation of processes of reflection "carried on within certain
groups toward which these processes have been directed."[22]
The third involves the selection of appropriate strategies
designed to secure the solution of tactical questions in the
conduct of political struggle. The object of the first function
is true statements; of the second, authentic insight; and of
the third, prudent decisions. Incidentally, as we shall later
see, Habermas believes falsely that these distinctions will
invalidate totalitarian political processes.

The reader will have noted by now, despite Habermas's
claim that intersubjective discussion will produce objective
knowledge, that his emphasis with respect to hermeneutics is
on consensus. Habermas undoubtedly has hit on one of
the key philosophical problems in the area of the objectivity
of knowledge. Truth cannot be demonstrated merely on the
basis of formal signs. For instance, we cannot "prove" to a
brain-damaged person that two plus two equals four, or to an
illiterate that the earth moves around the sun. Every proof
requires the reception of its truth by a person with adequate
capacity for understanding its terms and carrying out its
operations. "Proof" and "demonstration" are, after all, terms
employed by and applicable to human beings engaged in the
task of inquiry.

However, the distinction between a true and false consensus makes sense only on the basis of criteria that do not
refer to consensus. Thus, the doctors of Pasteur's time were

in consensus that Pasteur was wrong. There was nothing "inauthentic" about that consensus. The consensus, however, was incorrect.

When ordinary people disagree about simple matters, one aspect of judgment may involve the assertion that "X" is stupid or has brain damage. That is, a publicly communicable observation based on the standards of science determines that the person is incapable of carrying on logical operations. We know that dogs are color-blind because we observe their behavior but also because our metastatements about such observations will include a statement about the biological animal as an observing system with specific physiological characteristics.

Knowledge cannot be divorced from this interactive process. However, given the instrumentation—the person who interacts with others and with the environment—the standards are public. Their truth does not depend upon consensus—"authentic" or otherwise—although a consensus may emerge because of their truth. Thus, truth may be the possession of a single person. In this respect, there is no distinction between science, reflections about science, and praxis. Reflections about the theorems of science—and also about science and its methods—involve public tests. Thus, we reject the seventeenth-century philosophy of science because it cannot account for modern scientific knowledge.

It is true, as Habermas states, that the choice of primitive terms in a scientific system does not subject itself to the same form of proof as does the determination of whether an observation confirms or disconfirms a theory. However, the decision to accept Einstein's theory in place of Newton's—along with the differences in primitive terms and axioms employed by the former—rests on the fact that Einstein's theory "fits" the current realm of knowledge better than Newton's. Moreover, within this current framework of knowledge, Einstein's theory predicts observations that Newton's theory does not and also explains why Newton's theory is as accurate as it is within solar limits. These standards are public. They do not depend upon consensus.

Einstein's theory was not developed by a self-reflexive kind of hermeneutic reasoning. More likely, as most auto-biographies by scientists and mathematicians would lead us to believe, the development of theories is largely a pre-conscious process. However, this preconscious process ob-viously is illuminated by knowledge—for Einstein's theory presupposed knowledge of Michelson's experiments with light, the Lorentz equations, and neo-Euclidian geometries—and by some form of reasoning or assessment. Habermas's confusion on this subject perhaps stems from the well-known fact that the primitive terms of a theory together with its axioms provide the framework for explanation of the theory but are not themselves explained by the theory. However, as we have seen, this does not mean that they are not subject to scientific validation indirectly or that they cannot be ex-plained from other empirical frameworks. Their "truth" value rests on empirical test and consistency with other elements of the realm of knowledge and not on an *a priori* intersubjective consensus that is embedded in the structure of mind or language.

Allied errors are those of Noam Chomsky in linguistics, Claude Levi-Strauss in anthropology, and Edmund Husserl in philosophy. Although evolutionary adaption produced and favored a mental apparatus capable of appropriate syntactical and semantic operations prior to experience, explanations more likely than those of the former authors are available. Preconscious thought may employ a vocabulary and grammar more reliable but less precise than that of conscious thought, as John von Neumann speculated. The preconscious rules may adapt to experience through the development of alter-native grammatical and semantic rules. Or alternative rules or parts of rules may be available to the mind system depending on experience and/or internal stochastic processes. Once chosen, these possibly may feed back to the preconscious process. Any of the prior explanations will serve as preferable alternatives to that of Chomsky's or Levi-Strauss's deep structures—particularly because a system dependent on a strict one-to-one relationship between a deep structure and grammatical and/or semantic rules would be at an evolutionary disadvantage in coping with the great complexity of the world and with the novelties that confront humanity. Husserl's phenomenology makes an even more gross error—that of believing that because deductive applications of theory are dependent logically upon specific axioms and definitions, the structure of thought within which theories are developed and assessed is similar rather than having the characteristics of a field, as explained in the next chapter.

Other forms of reasoning do not require hermeneutical explanations either. For instance, if a physicist rejects mental telepathy, he will likely state that current physical theory is not able to account for the presumed quantity of energy that would be required. Significantly greater information indicating the validity of telepathy would lead to a search for a revision of physical theory consistent with it. Here the standards are those of consistency and "fit."

The difference of emphasis is fundamental. There is no fundamental self-reflexive form of argumentation or knowledge that gives its own guarantee of authentic consensus or truth. Public communicability, in Dewey's sense, always implies the presence of standards that permit public judgment on the basis of empirical test or some account of the consistency and "fit" of the realm of knowledge.

Although I shall not attempt a detailed argument here, Habermas in addition falls into a somewhat more sophisticated version of the difficulty that attended Rawls's theory in ethics. Habermas attempted to solve problems of praxis by distinguishing three spheres of action. In the sphere of truth, he says, there cannot be relations of domination, which he erroneously equates with authority. Therefore, he is for a share of student power in the schools. It is probably true that the best teachers attempt to enlighten their students through the power of their arguments. One object of teaching is to teach the student how to make inquiries on his own. But it does not follow from this that the student is the best judge of what he needs to know in order to accomplish this, or that he is fully capable of understanding the arguments that are being made. If this were really the case, it would be impossible to justify a distinction between teachers and students. Indeed, most students, for whatever reason, would be incompetent members of the faculty even after additional education and the passage of a number of years.

By the same token Habermas's extension of the argument for autonomy in the sphere of truth to the sphere of political action—no matter how much I am sympathetic to it in terms of my political values—will do nothing to invalidate an authoritarian movement. If one really believes that violent change of institutions is necessary to educate people for freedom—and that until this comes about they will be incompetent to understand their true interests—then a refusal to "coerce" the understanding of people will be regarded as irrelevant to real problems.

Although Habermas argues that only the past can be known scientifically and, hence, that there is no warrant for coercion, it is not correct that science cannot predict the unknown—quarks or gravitational waves, for instance. And although there are valid scientific arguments to support the claim that the first Communist revolution was a leap into the dark (see the argument in chapter 3 for the partial quality of knowledge in the social sciences), Habermas does not make them and pursues the principle past the point of legitimacy.

There is an alternative argument for coercion: an argument that Georg Lukacs accepted. He understood that Soviet Communism would employ terror and was not certain that its repressive apparatus ever would be dismantled. However, he argued privately that a failure to choose terroristic Communism was in effect a moral decision to accept a despicable status quo.

There are arguments against Lukacs's position including preferences for less efficient and therefore less permanent authoritarianisms, the evidence that Communist states are more resistant to change than democratic states, and inadequacies in Marxian theory. Habermas's argument, however, does not cut to the core of the moral problem that Lukacs thought he faced. Habermas salvages his humanism by turning praxis into an abstraction in which the conditions of life are divorced from the *a priori* transcendental distinctions that Habermas makes.

In the final analysis, despite his own reservations and subsequent efforts to substantiate his transcendental *a prioris* objectively, Habermas's hermeneutics remain subjective. Thus, his position remains defective. Although there is a self-reflexive (or recursive) process of thought, if communication is to occur among rational beings, this process must appeal not to a consensus but to the development of standards that permit public agreement. That not everything is measurable in the manner of the predictions of physical theory does not mean that publicly communicable standards are not available. If the dream of Marx concerning the demystification of social analysis is ever to be possible—a dream that sees the questing and self-conscious man as an integral part of the process— another path will have to be chosen.

Whereas Althuser remystifies the central Marxian concepts of economic relations and the forces of production, Habermas fails to demystify the process of public communication. Although he attempts to rescue normative political philosophy within the framework of a scientific approach, in the end he rests it upon a consensus determined by some mysterious self-reflexive thought process.

Language is treated by Habermas via the methods of the ordinary language school. Rather than a tool developed for human purposes and subject to restructuring depending upon its ability to accomplish the tasks for which it is employed, it becomes an obscure means for producing an "authentic" consensus.

Although I do not wish to pursue the point, the reader no doubt has already observed that Althuser and Habermas have retained a number of Marx's specific political and economic conclusions at a high price in terms of his general orientation. Althuser, by rejecting the early Marx, has retreated to a pre-Hegelian mechanistic conception of science in which man is largely absent except as an object. Habermas has attempted to save humanism by his use of hermeneutics. But this has driven him to a neo-Kantian transcendental *a priori*, albeit one that he says is approached via Hegel and hence that is dialectically enlightened.

Marx's comment on the withering away of the state emphasized his concern that men—real, individual, human beings—be in control of their own destinies. He neither foresaw nor could he have condoned the all-powerful "workers' " state. And, although workers' self-management, à la the Yugoslav experiment, likely would have appealed to Marx in principle, it does little, if anything, to break up the concentration of power in the modern socialist state that he likely would have abhorred. Marx also likely would not have been comfortable with revolutionary ideologies based on consensual *a priori*s rather than on publicly demonstrable theses. Such *a priori*s likely would have seemed to him a resurrection of a new holy family and of an old abstract concept of man.

Perhaps the efforts of Hegel and Marx to avoid dualism were predestined to failure. However, because I believe that they were dealing with central concerns of philosophy, I shall attempt to show how the solutions they devised and the problems they tried to resolve can be reformulated in a satisfactory manner.

Before turning to this task, however, I should like to suggest one additional reason—even if, for brevity's sake, in somewhat oversimplified form—for the problem Marx bequeathed to his posterity. Many writers have attempted to distinguish in Marx, as in Hegel, between the young and the old writer. Although I think this distinction is overstated—

being more a matter of emphasis than of differing principles—
it is interesting that the same development is found in each. I
believe the reason for this perhaps lies in the failure of each
writer to solve the basic philosophical problem with which he
was attempting to cope. And, as one aspect of their systems
seemed to lead toward extreme relativism, each recoiled
toward an identification of specific theories with all of reality.

I have already shown why this attempt fails: neither writer
is able to link his central logic to actual history. We have seen
how Althuser and Habermas attempt to solve this problem by
choosing opposite poles of the dilemma and how, pursuing
them to a logical extreme, they reach unadmitted but op-
posing anti-Marxian conclusions.

The root of the problem, which will be explored in the
next chapter, lies in epistemology. One Marx looks to the
concrete world of praxis for his philosophy. In his theses on
Feuerbach, he attacks contemplative philosophy and an-
nounces that the world is known by the changes we make in
it, by interaction with it. The other Marx harks back to a
unitarian theory of "truth" in which there is a real external
world that is copied by our senses. Hence truth is unique and
unchanging, and will be rediscovered as soon as the correct
class basis for knowledge is achieved. This is carried to its
extreme in Engels's *Origins of the Family,* where the future
but undelineated state of Communism is seen as a more
complex version of primitive communism. Apart from
Engels's unsophisticated understanding of so-called primitive
societies, this is essentially a fairy story in which the fairy
godmother (revolution) rescues the abducted princess (the
proletariat) and restores her to her kingdom, where she lives
happily forever after.

Our account clearly is invidious. Therefore, let me explicate the nature of the difficulty. Both Hegel and Marx faced
an apparently insoluble dilemma in the systems they were
building. If they rejected the idea of "truth," they were
driven to—and indeed, historically, had prepared the way

for—positivism, historicism, and extreme relativism. If they accepted the concept of truth—a dilemma that later became anguishing for George Lukacs—they were driven to a unitary system, the inner logic of which determined the world. Both Hegel and Marx came so close to a solution of this dilemma— the elimination of the ghost from the system concurrently with the maintenance of a second-order non-relativistic account of social problems and a first-order hierarchy of system preferences—that their failure is heartbreaking. The epistemological and analytical problems are the key to the solution and we now turn to them in the next two chapters.

Chapter 2

Resolution of the Epistemological Problem

The aim of chapters 2 and 3 is to resolve the metatheoretical problem that has been raised by those Marxian philosophers who have been concerned with the problem of alienation. I shall attempt to show that a systematic epistemological and theoretical analysis will resolve those major questions standing in the way of a scientific examination of normative questions and of questions of praxis as well. However, these publicly communicable, scientific methods will be adapted to their subject matters and will not be mere replicas of research methods in physics.

Pragmaticism

It is not so well known as it ought to be that Charles Sanders Peirce's pragmaticism, among its other objectives, sought to deal with the problem of knowledge that confronted the philosophical world after the breakdown of the Hegelian synthesis. Peirce was the one who did most to demystify the process. Peirce rejected the term "truth" as a characterization of empirical assertions because he associated the term with variations of the copy theory of knowledge. He therefore used "pragmaticism" as a covering term for what he called a theory of meaning. According to Peirce—and again I oversimplify—the meaning of something is revealed by the infinity of experiments we can conduct upon it.

Because of his experimental approach, Peirce has sometimes been accused of defining how something behaves but not what it is. This is misleading, for to refer to man as a rational being is meaningless unless we can specify what rational behavior is and predict that he will so behave under relevant conditions. Therefore, to call a man rational is equivalent to stating that he will be disposed to behavior that is rational in the circumstances of choice. This is the kind of information that is elicited by the series of experiments proposed by Peirce. And they do so within the consistently interactive framework—a framework in which natural beings interact with others within an environment—toward which Hegel and Marx pointed us.

I think that some of the confusion over the implications of Peirce's concept of "use" in experiments results from the simple view of "experiment" that most critics of Peirce have in mind. An infinite series of experiments would include metatheoretical experiments that would distinguish between the meaning of character,—which is dispositional and which can be analyzed only in terms of potential behavior in alternative circumstances,—and the meaning of an isolated or abstract instance of behavior. A sock in the jaw, for instance, is not an example of brutality if it is necessary to save a drowning swimmer. And running from a raging lion is not equivalent to abandoning one's wife to an unarmed rapist as an instance of cowardice. A proper series of experiments would probe the structures as well as the processes that determine behavior.

Because Peirce wrote before systems-analysis and communication-theory concepts were available, he could not use them in his analysis. It is the fusion of Peircean pragmaticism and systems analysis that I call systemic pragmaticism. Within its framework of analysis, I apply Peirce's method even more broadly than he did, and include the active experimenter and the experimental situation. This permits me to develop a philosophy of values and to meet some of the objections to his solution to the problem of knowledge.

The practitioners of pragmatism, most notably, Charles Peirce, John Dewey, and Morris Cohen, included among the aspects of life to be elucidated by pragmatic tests observable qualities of objects, relational aspects of being, and signs and symbols. Meaning is central, therefore, to pragmatism. Changes in the understanding of meaning occur through use.

As Morris Cohen so poignantly observed in his debates with Rudolf Carnap, every judgment concerning use, even with respect to so-called analytic statements, involves aspects of meaning not contained in the analytical system; for logical operations are possible only on the assumption that the "p" in one part of a logical statement is recognized as identical with the "p" in another part. As Quine demonstrated, we cannot construct a formal analytical system that does not depend on extrasystemic meaning, for such systems require knowledge of the meaning in use of "necessary," "includes," or some other analytical primitives that are extrasystemic. Nor can an evaluation of the adequacy of the operations of an analytical system be divorced from meaning in use. Particular observations are not related to observation sentences in a one-to-one fashion. Their interpretation, as Quine says, depends upon the corporate body of knowledge.

If we decide for relativity theory over Newtonian because it explains aspects of physical practice that the latter cannot, we also assess analytical systems in the same way. We learn through use that Aristotelian logic—in which we cannot prove that if a horse is an animal, the head of a horse is the head of an animal—does not exhaust the meaning of "analytical system" because we know that the head of a horse is the head of an animal. Whether we deal with "synthetic" or "analytical" aspects of knowledge, it is the use of communicative symbols that reveals meaning as we refine by cross-reference within the prior field of knowledge the relationships and references of the elements of the field. Thus, meaning in the pragmaticist sense is linked to objective knowledge, not ambiguously as Habermas links it in his discussion of the hermeneutic method, but intimately and in relationship to interactive experimental use.

This is true for the metatheories of science as for the specific theories of science. Thus, just as the "fit" of Einstein's theory with the corporate body of science of the time—and also its predicted observations—justify its replacement of Newtonian theory, the fact that the seventeenth-century theory of knowledge cannot account for the standards of proof successfully employed in modern physical theory accounts for the replacement of the older theory of science by recent theories of science. Evidence resulting from the successful work of scientists is used systematically, empirically, and objectively to validate conclusions both in the areas of theory and of metatheory. The criterion for validation of both theory and metatheory is not consensus, although it is assumed that properly trained critical minds possessed of the evidence will reach similar conclusions to the extent that the evidence is capable of clearly distinguishing between alternative hypotheses. The criteria in both cases refer to the evidence and the standards for its assessment, not to consensus.

What is the fundamental way in which Peircean pragmaticism demystifies the methodology initiated by Hegel and pursued by Marx? Both Hegel and Marx fused theory and metatheory: that is, specific theory and realm of praxis. In the Peircean methodology, metatheory—that is, the general framework of interpretation of the current realm of science—determines the content of theory only by excluding theories that are inconsistent with well-confirmed aspects of the realm of knowledge. It does not operate at a level of detail that permits the determination of univocal "true" theories independently of a rich inquiry into the specific subject matter to which the specific theory applies. Although a modern philosophy of science will explain why alchemy is an unacceptable theory, it cannot be used to determine which of the current rival scientific theories is correct—for example, the theory that gravity is weakening or the theory that it is constant.

In the social sciences an appropriate metatheory will not decide for or against capitalism or socialism. Metatheory shows how the framework of inquiry can exclude many theories that fail to "fit" the modern frame of knowledge. However, more specific results in theory require more specific investigations, for example, of class relationships in different societies.

We have seen in the preceding chapter how the attempt to fuse metatheory to the determination of theoretical results produced a disjunction between specific concrete analysis and the general framework of analysis in Marxian theory. Such a fusion was more appropriate, although it did not work even there, in idealistic Hegelian philosophy, for idealism at least presumes that the world is derived from Idea. If, however, we start from a framework of pragmaticistic interaction between the subject and the environment, we are dealing with a world in which there is not even a semiplausible reason for metatheory to determine the truth statements of theory. Only when we realize this will we have achieved the demystification that Marx unsuccessfully sought.

In the years since Peirce wrote, the concept of truth has lost the meaning that led him to abandon it. Thus, I do not reject use of the term, although I mean by "truth" what Peirce meant by "meaning." Peirce wrote before the development of communication theory. Although Peirce and others of his persuasion recognized values as genuine aspects of the world, this made it difficult for them to demonstrate the intimate relationship between the interactive approach and a scientific assessment of the problem of values. In the remainder of this chapter, I shall show how an appropriate epistemology that uses communication theory concepts and applies them to a transfinitely stable concept of the person can treat values as scientifically as so-called ordinary facts. I shall then show in chapter 3 how a metatheory of social science invalidates other mistakes of the Marxians: the use of one single global theoretical framework for social analysis and the treatment of problems of praxis by the methods of theory. I shall also show how this metatheory of social science permits the objective treatment of other subjects that were called into question by the sociology of knowledge and how the dichotomy between the nomothetic and the ideographic mistakes the character of scientific inquiry. My examination of these subjects, albeit brief, is meant to demystify both the metatheory of social science and the subject matter of alienation.

"Circularity" in Knowledge

The analysis of meaning is "circular" in some respects, for there necessarily is an appeal from one form of statement involving meaning to another. Circularity is evident whenever we try to exhaust meaning by an analysis involving epistemology. Observations always involve relations among the observer, that which is observed, and the context of observation. Attempts to exhaust these always force the observer to consider the matter from some other standpoint, which, in turn, is not observed.

We use our human senses to observe instruments that are then used to assess the human physiology, and so forth. The eye and the hand construct the ruler, which then is used for measurement; and the measurements are then observed by humans. Time, length, color, and so on, are characteristics not of objects alone but of objects, contexts, and measuring instruments. The complete system can never be examined within the same framework; for the attempt to do so establishes a new framework of examination in which the former is treated as an element of the experiment. The entire system is dependent upon preexisting knowledge, for neither a person nor a computer could transform a signal into data except on the basis of a code for interpretation. This is the basic but misleading truth that underlies the Platonic observation that nothing can be learned and that we merely remember what we had forgotten.

The true starting point of inquiry is not doubt or even thought, for they depend upon the existence of a problem. It is experience; not of experience in general or of being in general but of experience of particular beings, "things," or relationships. It is the attempt to account for experience that transforms some experienced beings or "things" into objects of thought. And it is thought about this that transforms particular thoughts into objects of thought. It is because we are particular kinds of beings that we are capable of thinking and of doubting, that is, of treating a thought as an object of thought.

The transformation of either an experience or of a thought into an object of thought is the means by which one thinking being can communicate linguistically with another. Thought as an object of thought is always localized as the thought of a particular being at a particular time and in a particular place. Thinking about the thought can never be localized in the same way except insofar as it is objectified at some other mental level. This process is recursive; and it is the failure to recognize the recursive aspect of this process that gives rise to the illusion of a transcendental ego. That which is not an object of thought is not subject to the categories of thought, unless, in turn, it is subjected to the recursive process of thinking; for it is only through the application of categories that experiences are transformed into thoughts or statements about identifiable objects. However, there is no transcendental subjective ego that lies beyond this process, as we are dealing with different phases of the same experiential process.

It is not clear that our knowledge of our existence as a self is inferred from experience, for experience would be impossible without some inherent coding system; and the initial coding might distinguish between the self and its environment. However, our identification of the boundaries and the character of the self clearly is inferred from experience. Among other things, we note that covering our eyes interferes with vision, that as we walk our experience of our surroundings changes, that when we sleep the nature of our experience changes, and so forth. The experiences hypothesized as external are then related to our experiences of ourselves. We then hypothesize a particular kind of physical constitution to account for these experiences. The kind of being we are is then differentiated from other kinds of beings. We observe similarities between ourselves and other beings that we identify as of the same type, and differences from others with whom our identifications are weaker or non-existent.

Solipsism is irrelevant and there is no ghost in the system. The concept of a transcendental ego confuses the process of organizing experiences with an independent ground for experience that cannot be investigated by the methods of science. Kant's difficulty was that he was insufficiently familiar with recursive processes and that he failed to understand that it was the recursive process of transforming thoughts into objects of thought that provided the illusion of a transcendental ego; an ego that, if not entirely beyond the process, somehow possessed an unchanging and *a priori* relationship to it.

The mistake of the ordinary language philosophers who succeeded Wittgenstein was to identify the process by means of which a community of scientists comes to accept particular criteria for valid statements with the validity of the criteria. Although language is required for communication and science, language is merely a tool for investigating phenomena and may be restructured and adapted—although only slowly if our language base is to retain its capacity as a tool—both as our understanding of problems changes and as the problems themselves are different. Although our recognition of the inadequacy of particular tools of language and method cannot be communicated to ill-prepared or inadequately structured receptors, the criterion of choice is that of validity, not of consensus.

The world of science is the world of the object language. It employs categories and its models are closed. It applies equally to the physical and to the human; for, in principle, we can model the recursive process that characterizes human thought even if we currently know so little about it that our attempts are clumsy and primitive. The inadequacies of behavioristic psychology result not from its use of scientific methods but from its failure to recognize the recursive elements in the psychic processes by means of which meaning is attributed to situations and from its failure to employ adequate models.

However, "adequate model" does not imply an accurate existential prediction. The predictions of "hard" service are by and large existentially accurate because the system parameters are seldom subject to flux and because most of the system variance that is important to the human experimenter is captured by the model. Nonetheless, the concrete world of experience is always open. It is never captured entirely by the models and categories of thought we apply to it. Predictions always apply within the framework of models and of sentences employing property terms. The world of experience, the concrete, real world, is never entirely reducible to the categories of communication and of science. The problems that pursue us philosophically stem from the recurrent attempts to identify the process of being with the objectified world of science. These two worlds are related but not identical. The latter is a tool for finding one's way within the former. It is a tool that purchases its power at the price of at least partial "misrepresentation." There is no magical form of hermeneutics that will close this "circle." We can narrow the gap, however, by specifying at a metatheoretical level the techniques that permit a multifaceted, but not unitary, approach to the problem of analysis, as we will in chapter 3.

The entire process of inquiry takes place within a field of knowledge, all the elements of which have meaning. This applies to primitive terms, concepts and definitions, axioms, propositions, and theories. The entire field is in a rough sort of "floating" equilibrium, the "balance" or consistency or "fit" of which determines the criteria of identification and evidence that we employ and the confirmation of experimental results that we reach. The process is "circular" in the sense that we can never go outside of the field in making a judgment and that no elements of the field constitute criteria for the remainder of the field without in turn being subject to criteria elsewhere in the field. However, the process is objective in two senses. In the large sense, we can specify why our choices of identifications and standards of proof "fit" together on the basis of evidence or why they do not and, hence, why some of the elements of the field require alteration. In the small sense, we accept parts of the field as "givens" in conducting our experiments and in evaluating their results. These experiments bring new information into the field and even though the coding of this information is determined by some of the prior elements of the field, it may be inconsistent with other elements of the field. As these experiments call into question at least some of the "givens," we begin to rearrange the field. The standards are objective, publicly communicable, and developed in use as Peirce used that term.

Some failures in the application of scientific methods in the realm of human affairs stem not from the correctly perceived "intentionality" of much of human action but from the failure to appreciate the differences between mechanical and homeostatic systems. Thus, the application of terms and measurements to different types of social systems, as if their meaning were identical regardless of context, produces the error of overabstraction.

Whereas most of the theoretically defined terms in physical science, such as energy, can be given a definite and general meaning for a wide variety of contexts—and whereas statements concerning their equality or inequality are generally valid—terms such as "father" or units of such factors as "gross national product" are usually too crude to be applied directly and uniformly to different types of social or political systems.

The meanings of scientific terms change over time as more is learned concretely about science. Usually, however, the terms of science remain general—perhaps with some shift in scope—whereas changes in the meanings of the terms of social science usually involve major changes in range or scope of application and greater differentiation in use than is true of science.

The error of overabstraction, however, also characterizes some philosophies of science that, for instance, reify the general concept of "measurement," for "measuring," as distinguished from the measurement of particular theoretically defined terms, does not have identical meaning in different physical science spheres. This is the sense in which we learn "what science is from what scientists do," provided that the phrase is not taken literally, in which case we could not distinguish good science from bad science. It is the expansion of scientific activity into different realms that enlightens our understanding of science by revealing similarities and differences.

The failure to distinguish between a scientific theory (explanatory framework) and the realm of knowledge within which it is interpreted (realm of praxis or assessment) leads to the mistake in which the characteristics of theory are attributed to the entire realm of scientific knowledge. Thus, the requirement for a set of initial axioms—a requirement that does apply to a theory—is falsely attributed to the entire body of knowledge. However, the latter is a realm of praxis rather than of theory; and its elements reinforce each other in a loose equilibrium, in which considerations of consistency, economy, and so forth determine the elements that are tentatively held constant and those that are tentatively varied.

Fundamental axioms have been altered—for instance, no action at a distance—when inconsistent with an economical theory. Observations are disbelieved—for instance, the statistical evidence for telepathy—in the absence of a theory consistent with theories of physics that will explain them. Standards of evaluation are changed—the distinction between warm and cold—when confronted with theoretical requirements for a concept such as temperature. Even more revolutionary changes in the most "solid" aspects of scientific belief will change if the "loose" equilibrium of the realm of knowledge (praxis) requires this.

Moreover, there is the problem of identification of observations. Is a noise a belch? If it is a belch, is it evidence of bad manners, as in the United States, or of politeness after a meal, as in the Orient? Is it a hallucination of a defensive personality? Is it a scrape of a shoe which is misinterpreted by such a personality? Is a Portuguese man-of-war one animal or a colony? Is a man whose cortical hemispheres have been bisected one person or two? These are not perceived as simple facts. Predispositions, whether empirical or theoretical, determine perceptions. Yet perceptions can be tested only against other perceptions. The determination of what is held constant and what is permitted to vary in this perceptual process depends upon the loose equilibrium of the realm of praxis.

Some humanistic psychologists following Maslow speak of peak experiences that are accessible only to those who have peak experiences and that—as in the case of ordinary scientific observations, as they perceive that process—are validated by consensus among those who have such experiences. They are correct in perceiving that science never escapes the circle of experience. Depending upon what is meant by "peak experiences," they may be correct in believing that these "exist." However, if by "peak experiences" they mean something other than satisfaction of an emotional kind or aesthetic harmony; if they imply a hypothesis concerning the human condition in other senses; then, if what they say is valid, it must be consistent with the other elements of the loose equilibrium of the field of knowledge. Even if there are elements of the "peak" experience that cannot be conveyed to one who has not had it, one should be able to explain it as one might explain sight to a blind person, including the consistency of the visual experience with tactile experiences. Consensus alone will not validate a peak experience, for it may be produced by a consensus of emotion- or drug-induced states of mind that have no external referent.

No theory can be permitted to determine its own conditions of truth; this would be genuinely circular. Rather, all circumscribed aspects of the field of knowledge must be tested for consistency, "fittingness," and partial relatedness with all others. However, this testing itself invokes other theories, propositions, and observations.

The distinction between theory and praxis is not absolute. They function as partly, although not completely, successive phases in inquiry. This is circular but not visciously so, for the circulation of phases involves not a constant pool of knowledge but a "deepening" and expanding pool.

A similar process occurs in the realm of values; and that is why the comparative test in principle—rather than the effort to discover a single system of morals that is general for all societies and environments—is the correct approach. The latter mistake replicates the error of overabstraction found in some mistaken philosophies of science and social science theories.

Values and Objectives

Chapter 6 analyzes the human person as a transfinitely stable goal-seeking system. In principle, we can analyze its behavior and infer its values by means of that analysis. We infer its good from the purposeful system's choice of goals.[1] (Chapter 1 of *Justice, Human Nature, and Political Obligation* investigates the characteristics of transfinitely stable systems in a manner that is intended to justify this conclusion. The discussion in chapter 6 of the sacred reproduces some of this argument.)

If we characterize the valuable as that which would be judged good in the presence of correct information, we can distinguish between what is valued and the valuable. If "ought" statements are taken out of the elliptical imperative form, "X ought to do g," they would appear as "X ought to do g because g has the consequence h, which is valuable for X," or as "X ought to do g because g has the consequence j which is valuable for Y, the good of whom is valuable for X."

The statement by a person as to what he values is evidence of what is valuable for him; but it is rebuttable evidence. Note that this type of system can produce objectively definable pathological behavior. Suppose a person is in an extremely unfavorable environment. He may have to forgo important needs. Since this is unpleasant, mechanisms of denial may operate. We will now show that this process of valuation is as objective as the natural language use of colors.

"This is yellow" and "This is a dove" are elliptical expressions. "This is yellow" stands for "This is seen as yellow by such and such an observational system in such and such a type of lighting and in the absence of such and such types of filters, atmospheric or otherwise."

Each statement of the type "This is yellow" or "This is a dove" implies something about an observer, an object or event external to the observer, and the context of observation. In the common language, commonsense distinctions are made between "is" and "appears." If we are incautious, these can lead to reifications that produce false conclusions.

There is an important distinction between "dove" and "yellow" with respect to the "is/appears" disjunction. Although a piece of flying paper at a distance may appear to be a dove, the tests that can be performed to confirm the distinction between "is" and "appears" are consistent with an extremely wide range of contextual circumstances and observational systems. The distinction between "is" and "appears" with respect to color, however, depends upon a conventional stipulation of a specific type of observational context.

Although, for reasons obvious to the conditions of life in the solar system, a different conventional standard would be absurd in practice, it is not absurd in principle. Moreover, although unlikely for evolutionary reasons, in principle the observational system might report differently when in different states, as it does with respect to tastes for food. Differently evolved creatures might report differently. And these differences in reports would not be merely linguistic differences, for there would be a difference in observations. In principle these differences in observation could be confirmed objectively by operations on the physiologies of the two species that transform one into the other and that then reverse the process. In this case, a statement that reported that "X is yellow" would not permit second-order agreement on the referent X without specification of the instrument (observational system) used in making the report.

With respect to the good, this aspect of a report is essential, for the report is meaningless except for the relationship between the observing system and the context in which the observation is made. Thus, just as "X is yellow" is not invariant for two beings with different perceptual systems, "X is good" is not invariant regardless of context and system state.

We can distinguish between "X is good" and "X appears good," for we can relate the distinction to the information possessed by the person in the context of his human and other natural relationships. Moreover, this distinction is not merely a convenient convention, as in the specification of "in light with the characteristics of Sol I" for color. It refers to an actual difference in the world for which the attribution of goodness has relevance just as "biological animal" does for the case of dove. In both cases criteria govern the decision. As these criteria are applied and developed in different contexts, we become aware of differences and similarities in different kinds of goods as well as of more central types of goods such as justice. These further discriminations lead to knowledge of more general kinds of goods, although their relationships and character will vary with system contexts.

Because the copy theory of knowledge mistakes this process, the distinction between values and other types of facts to which it gives rise is incorrect. There is no external "color" or "size" to which an internal representation corresponds. Nor are values subjective because they do not refer to corresponding external objects. Instead there is a differentiated field of knowledge that presents some events as internal to a person and others as external. And every hypothesis that serves as a potential explanation of either employs categories that presume interactions between a person and his environment that produce the categories in terms of which an explanation is offered. Each such hypothesis is confirmed or disconfirmed by contemporaneous or subsequent elements of the field of knowledge or experience.

If assertions concerning the valuable refer at least in part to processes internal to the person, so do psychological and physiological explanations. Even if the latter made no reference to factors outside the person—and this is counterfactual—they would differ from valuations only in terms of the categories of explanation and not in terms of location. Thus, location inside the self does not make an explanation subjective even according to the ordinary usage that still carries over from the earlier epistemology that presumed a dichotomy between a real external and objective world—at least in terms of primary categories such as space and time if not in terms of perceptual categories such as color—and an internal, subjective world of representations.

This process is circular only in the philosophically universal sense that we cannot account for any information or knowledge, except on the assumption that the perceiving system starts with information or knowledge. This applies to information concerning both so-called ordinary facts and values.

Learning involves negative feedback; and this necessitates that at least some of the initial state of information be adequate for the correction of other elements. Thus, beliefs about the valuable will be altered as more is learned about man and his environment.

Many major rearrangements have occurred in value systems. Usually, these are triggered by social or economic changes that force major readjustments of important institutions. Sometimes changes in knowledge help produce them; sometimes mistakenly so, as in the case of the inferences from relativity, quantum mechanics, and Freudian theory that many have made about the nature of man.

Conclusions concerning all cannot be fitted into or derived from a single theory. But reasons can be offered for the consistency of the field. Thus, it might be shown that certain social changes are inconsistent with certain valued consequences or that these consequences are not really desired in the new circumstances. The test in principle and comparative knowledge permit ordered choices concerning preferences that relate them to the interactions of a transstable human nature with actual existential circumstances rather than to a mere subjective adjustment on the basis of immediate possibility. Therefore, we turn to the test in principle.

The Test in Principle

The test in principle was presented first in the introductory essay of *Macropolitics:*

Consider a situation in which a man would be able to relive his past in thought. He could be confronted with each of the branching points of his major life decisions and allowed subjectively to live the alternative lives. If individual choices could be tested in this fashion, social and political and moral choices could be tested in analogous fashion by confrontations with different patterns of social, political, and moral organization under different environmental constraints.

Presumably this would confront men with choices that are meaningful. Thus, where the material environments of the social and political systems were presented as "givens," the individual would observe the consequences of different positionings and different circumstances within the systems. He could observe which roles he would prefer if he could choose his roles and how much he would like or dislike the system if roles were chosen for him. Within his own life patterning, he could compare choices over those things where he in fact had the freedom to choose differently. Within these constraints, his conceptions of the good depend upon the limitations of institutional life and environment. In the second form of testing, he could vary institutional life and material environment, again in two ways. He could compare systems as to which he would prefer if he could choose his role and which he would prefer if his role were assigned to him. On the basis of a more limited freedom, he could compare differences in the existing institutional structures with respect to his past decision points, where he had some freedom to effect changes in them.

After experiencing these alternatives, the individual would return to his actual situation. He would then have to choose in the present on the basis of the limited alternatives available to him. He now has a standard against which to judge his practicable choices; if he has interdependent utilities, it will be too uncomfortable for him not to make some effort to move the system closer to alternatives that are practicable, not too deprivational for him, and better for others as well. Presumably he will not confuse himself about the harm he does to others because of his needs under existing constraints.

If these suggestions seem too fantastic, we could consider the more limited kinds of comparisons that we in fact make when we talk about propositions of this kind. These do not have the fullness of comparison suggested above and they suffer from the defect that we are constrained by our own local conditions in making comparisons. None the less we can and do make at least limited comparisons and occasionally we even decide against our own social system on this basis, as many Germans did during the time of Nazi Germany. The degree of confidence to be placed in such localized comparisons must be quite low, for we do not fully know upon what conditions the system consequences are dependent. However, our ability to relate positions to life and social experiences is itself a solvent and does produce a broader set of comparisons. In any event, our conception of the nature of man as a valuating system is meaningful, the conception of limits to plasticity and costs for wrong choices is meaningful, and, therefore, at a minimum the concept of local comparisons is meaningful.[2]

There is one other form of empirical testing that in principle sheds light on our problem. Individuals confronted with evidence that would militate against particular practices that are to their benefit in existing social and environmental circumstances presumably would be forced into pathological processing of information because of their need to avoid empathetic knowledge of the harm they are doing to individuals whose needs or rights they would otherwise be forced to recognize. We are rarely confronted with desperate choices of this kind because the process of socialization produces both the expectation that certain reward structures are justified and inattention to the deprivations they entail. As a consequence, individuals do not have to divert their attention from the deprivations of others; they are on the whole not aware of them. However, where such information is presented to the individual, presumably it would generate information-processing pathologies and these would give rise to cognizable physiological disturbances.

This suggestion is offered hesitantly, for I fully recognize the immense difficulty of attempting to validate a particular explanation of an informational disturbance of this kind. Moreover, in social systems that are sufficiently pathological, it would be the empathetic individual who recognizes injustice who might manifest the most disturbance. However, although the empathetic individual would suffer in most actual situations because of his greater sensitivity to information, in principle we could show that it is his cognition of, or at least his belief concerning, the ways in which current conditions deprive other individuals that produces the pathology. Presumably by forcing others to confront data of this kind, we could also produce similar pathologies in them.

Values and Praxis

Knowledge, whether of science or of the valuable, exists as a field that is constantly readjusted to changes rather than as a single deductive system, whether normative or non-normative. Thus value judgments are not deduced from normative rules, from factual elements, or from assessments of good outcomes. Rather, these coexist in a loose "balance" in arriving at value judgments. This field of praxis is not predetermined by an intersubjectively recognized "authentic" set of transcendental primitive terms and assumptions. The field must operate on a code that permits corrections. In the process, and over time, the field may be entirely, or almost entirely, restructured. This restructuring is justified in part by normal scientific methods for testing theories and propositions and in part by a publicly communicable recognition of "fit" and consistency. The latter constitutes praxis.

The test in principle is in the area of praxis and permits an individual to detach himself from his "accidental" setting in making judgments. It is sufficiently contextual to permit meaningful moral judgments in deciding upon political activity in seeking change. Thus, an individual does not have to attach himself blindly or unreasonably to any social class or "motor" of history. His judgmental process remains rational. Although he is detached from blind adherence, a framework is established that permits a reasoned and ordered attachment to causes and, thus, to an avoidance of alienation. This is an objective, scientific process and is quite different from Habermas's hermeneutics.

First- and Second-Order Values

The subjective variants of Marxian thought propose a world in which conflict and alienation are absent. For reasons given earlier in this chapter, this reintroduces the mystical kernel into Marxian doctrine. We will now show why a proper interactive analysis—of the type Marx attempted but did not accomplish—would indicate the partial character of human identifications. For this purpose, we will use an analogy from physics to draw a distinction between first- and second-order concepts of objectivity with respect to values. Both second- and first-order objectivity in values are relevant to a conception of justice. To illustrate the difference between the two concepts, we will employ the clock "paradox" of Einsteinian relativity theory. According to this theory, an observer on each of two systems moving with respect to the other will observe time on the other system as going more slowly. Common sense tells us that it is contradictory to believe that time in each system can be moving more slowly with respect to time in the other system. Yet, because of the relativity of motion with respect to independent inertial systems, an observer in each observes time on the other to be moving more slowly. Each observer, if he is familiar with relativity theory, will recognize that his opposite number on the other system is reaching conclusions that mirror his and will understand why he does so from his frame of reference. Thus, we have a second-order system within which objective and non-contradictory statements are made concerning what the two observers observe. On the other hand, the "truths" of the two observers on different inertial systems lack a common point of reference that permits first-order agreement concerning the two systems.

If, on the other hand, a twin enters a spaceship, flies out into space, and returns, biological measurements will establish that he is younger than the twin who remained on earth. In this case, however, the twin who went into space needed to accelerate to leave the gravitational pull of the earth and to return to it. The fact of acceleration was observable by physical instrumentation and measurable. The system that accelerates is known to move with respect to another system and, therefore, the former Einsteinian constraint does not apply. The twin who goes into space expects to be younger than the twin who remains on earth. Common measurements made by both predict and confirm this fact. The apparent paradox arises only with respect to systems that are on independent inertial paths. The observers who share a common universe also share a common framework of first-order objective, physical truth.

The reader is already familiar with our argument that values are generated as the consequence of the interactions of transfinitely stable persons with other persons in real environments. The analogy with Einsteinian relativity, although partial, is genuine. Time-space coordinates in Einsteinian theory give rise to measurements only from the standpoint of the interactive observer. This produces the disjunction between the conclusions of observers on different inertial systems, although each conclusion is objectively given by each observer's framework of reference and each observer will know what conclusions the other will reach. Placement in an inertial system is a historical fact. Similarly the existential identifications of the valuing person with other individuals, groups, or organizations constitute the focus for establishing a first-order framework of justice. There are always some conflicting interests; and sometimes these conflicts in interest are so great that no first-order framework exists.

If two independently inertial systems somehow coalesce into a single inertial system, first-order as well as second-order objective statements thereafter would become possible for the observers. Our theory of justice implies that this is what occurs as the extension of identification among individuals and among systems produces a common frame of reference within which common first- as well as second-order objective statements have validity. The analogy is not exact, however, for existential circumstances may break this bond for particular individuals within systems or may attenuate it to the point of extreme ambivalence with respect to the requirements of just behavior.

This also explains the seeming paradox of conflict of values that Mannheim incorrectly called "bias." The test in principle may permit a weakly ordered set of evaluations for alternative political and social systems common to all men much as the Einsteinian relativity equations are common for observers on different inertial systems. However, just as the Einsteinian relativity equations are consistent with mirror-imaged estimations of movement by the different observers, the common set of social and political evaluations is consistent with different evaluations of appropriate paths to them or of conflicting interests on the way that are generated by different existential loci. The gap between interests is thus a recurrent source of alienation.

To understand this problem better, let us examine briefly the differences and similarities between the use of relative frames of reference in Einsteinian physics and the use of a similar concept in ethics. The space traveler can be in one and only one inertial system at a time. Individuals may identify with themselves, with other individuals, or with one or more social systems. Whether any solution is possible in a given set of circumstances that produces "good" results from all frameworks of reference is a factual matter. Even if this is possible, it will still be necessary in most cases to compromise the good from one or more standpoints. If it is not possible, the strength of the individual's identifications will determine which framework of reference will be sacrificed.

Empirical measures for frameworks of identification, even though of low confidence, are possible, much as a psychologist may determine whether or not a person is projecting. However, these determinations are made by weighing evidence from a variety of areas; and terms are used whose meanings are at least partly determined by the contexts in which they are employed. The meanings and measurements are not determined by an overriding theory employing terms for which universal measures are available as in the case of physics. This thrusts the problem into the area of praxis. Further, the fact that "solutions" involve adjustments among frames of reference, rather than derivation from a unique perspective, emphasizes criteria of consistency and adjustment, key elements of the arena of praxis. This is still within the ambit of science—for the selection of axioms and definitions within theory is determined in part by the "praxis" framework of science, including consistency with other theories and propositional information—and hence of objectivity, at least in Dewey's sense of public communicability. The understanding of this partly explains the error in attempting to reduce ethics to a theory with a universal set of rules that governs all situations and all individuals.

Let us now distinguish what objectivity means in terms of the test in principle. We repeat that we are not asserting that we have in fact carried out a test in principle. The moral order is probably only weakly ordered. Individuals, in any system, will have a weakly ordered preference for roles in that system. This preference order will depend upon information and environmental conditions. Within any system, individuals will have a weakly ordered preference for the individual values that characterize the system's cultural norms. These preferences will depend upon information and conditions. Individuals will have a weakly ordered set of preferences for alterations in any system. These will depend on information and conditions. Individuals will have a weakly ordered set of preferences for other types of systems. These preferences will depend on information and conditions. Individuals will have a weakly ordered set of preferences for alternative environmental conditions. These will depend on roles, systems, and information. The complete set of weak orderings will establish an ordered hierarchy of preferences. It may be invariant. However, we can carry the weak ordering one step farther and it will remain consistent with objectivity. Let us assume that under conditions of the test in principle, some agree that some societies are among the worst and some are among the best, but that they differ in other comparative evaluations. We would call the latter personal or idiosyncratic and the former second-order objective aspects of the problem. The fact that not all aspects of moral orderings were subject to even second-order evaluations would not erase the existence of those aspects that are subject to either first- or second-order rankings.

Let us now state how second-order criteria are used to determine an invariant order for changes within systems or for transitions between them. The second-order criteria for choice will be determined by step functions. By this I mean that any significant alteration in conditions or systems will trigger a new constellation or ordering of values. The possibility of such change will bring to consciousness the possibility of such a new ordering as a guide to decision. Because the order is weak, some alternatives may not be morally distinguishable, although the relationship of values in each will be different. Because this process is related to actual choice conditions, the potentially best set (or sets) of values do not govern moral choices, except possibly as a minor qualifier so as not unnecessarily to foreclose it as a future possibility. Nor is this required for objectivity, because we have an invariant guide for relevant transition states in terms of moral equivalents. Reasons do determine the choice of transition values; for instance, as there is no longer a shortage of resources, the values associated with such shortages are inappropriate. However, the area is one of praxis, and the "fit" of the realm of knowledge rather than a single theory is determinative. Hence, no unique theory will permit the derivation of uniquely appropriate reasons.

Objectivity and Human Nature

These preference orderings represent dispositions of humans under different conditions. By human nature I mean the dispositional ordering established by the ordered hierarchy outlined in the previous section.

One other possibility may be mentioned. Hereditary physiological differences may produce temperament differences that in turn produce differences in what is valuable. This does not reduce objectivity, for we can still produce an invariant moral hierarchy for each physiological type. As this ordering becomes weaker, however, the identification of the different types will weaken. It may become so tenuous that no common moral universe will exist for them. This will produce a variant of the frame-of-reference problem discussed in chapter 3.

One variant of the test in principle may be applicable even in this case—a variant in which individuals compare the preferences for moral rules that they would have, depending upon their physiologies and upon their preferences for physiological types. This might permit recognition of a "best" type or, at least, of "better" types. Almost surely this would be the case for those whose "crippling" is obvious, as in the case of those who have undeveloped physical parts or brain damage. Although existential identifications would still produce conflict over moral principles, common recognition of "best" or "better" would serve as a modifying agent that restores some common moral ground.

Praxis and the Chain of Being

Part 2 of this book explicates alienation from an ontological point of view. Some readers, however, may feel some discomfort—although others surely will not—in the apparent separation of human beings from the chain of being. To attempt to make this bridge would be speculative, and perhaps excessively so. Yet, because it is relevant, I shall accept this risk and touch upon the matter, if only briefly.

In *On Freedom and Human Dignity,* I quoted and commented on an early position I took in *Macropolitics:*

> If "all organic material were multistable, or at least ultrastable, then all organic material would have regulatory components. If this were so, it would be possible for such systems to regulate not only to maintain the value of some essential variable but also to increase some aspect of it. This selectivity need not be intelligent. In the earlier forms of organic life structural changes might occur as a consequence of random mutation. There might, however, be selectivity based not merely on efficiency with respect to environmental adaptation but also with respect to the satisfaction of the programmed regulatory goals of the system. If this were the case, then there might even be a hierarchical order in [but not of] the universe, not as matter of necessity or of law, but in the sense of certain tendencies toward this ordering" [*Macropolitics,* pp. 47-48].

If there is no direct evidence to support this hypothesis, neither is there any evidence, including that stated by [Jacques] Monod, to invalidate it. This tendency, if it existed, would be purposive, although not in the self-reflexive sense of conscious thought. It would be entailed in the coding of the organism. This speculation could be carried a step further than I carried it in *Macropolitics*. Neither ultra- nor multistability would be possible in inorganic nature. However, there could be an inherent tendency—defeatable by untoward circumstances—toward the stabilization of chance configurations at the inorganic level that increased the probability somewhere in the system of [the formation of] organic molecules containing an ultrastable coding. Or, even if ultrastability were absent in the initial organic compounds, there could be a coding that maintained this probability until ultrastability developed. Although the circumstances that led to these formations would be accidental, their appearance would not be improbable in cosmic terms.[3]

A different but analogous conception is offered by J. M. Burgers:[4]

In [Alfred North] Whitehead's picture the Universe is not just matter and motion, but is a complex of processes which inceasingly are evaluating forms of relationship and which express the results of these evaluations in facts and in structures. Tradition evidently is a strong rule in the majority of cases, as we perceive when we think of the enormous amount of nonliving matter in the Universe. Nevertheless, traditions are not absolute. Exceptions to the rigidity of traditions are possible, and new initiatives may spring up, giving room for changes and new traditions. This is where life is supposed to have emerged.

Although Burgers is careful in his article not to introduce anthropomorphic meanings into his use of "initiative," "evaluation," "memory," "tradition," and "anticipation," or to imply the possibility of natural selection at the inorganic level, his vocabulary is troublesome. Whether anticipation can have any meaning in the absence of a "control" system seems doubtful to me. Moreover, his interesting speculation that the regular behavior we observe even in microphysical particles may have developed out of more random behavior in which certain "preferred" behaviors became stabilized over time does not require his vocabulary. A microcoding might produce the same result; and such a microcoding would not be among the axioms employed in specific physical theories, for they are formulated to account for the regularities that preceded the advent of man. Obviously, either thesis— Burgers's or mine—is so speculative that it has little value in the narrow sense of theory. From the standpoint of praxis— the realm of knowledge—however, each may have more value than the "chance" hypothesis because it "fits" better with more elements of the realm of knowledge.

Moreover, the concept of chance, as it is used in ordinary discourse, is ambiguous. That seeds grow into plants is not accidental if a greenhouse is assumed as the environment. Were outer space the environment, the development would be impossible. That a particular person is born is a chance event if only the intercourse of the parents is specified. If the characteristics of the particular sperm and ovum are specified, the matter is no longer accidental. That some fish eggs will become fish is likely if one specifies the large production of eggs by fish. However, that a particular spawn lives to become a fish in a "hostile" environment—the "normal" environment of spawn—is an accident, unless one makes microspecifications in which case it is no longer an accident. According to our speculation, the development of human life from inorganic matter is an accident if one attempts to predict the history of the path from a specific starting state. If, however, one attempts to predict only the general form of the development, then, although the specific path is produced by a series of events, each of which has very low probability in any properly selected time frame, the emergence of intelligent life, although not necessarily in a particular configuration, is virtually inevitable. And the universe, rather than being hostile in Monod's sense, is a benign environment that permits life's emergence. Whether emerging levels of organization are "anticipated" in Burgers's sense or encoded and self-stabilizing in the sense of my hypothesis, an emerging level of organization is not derivable from a theory accounting for the prior level, although it must not be inconsistent with the constraints imposed by that level.

Let us momentarily return to "information" and "memory." A coin has "memory" in the sense that it retains its shape over time. That shape may also be regarded as information. However, "memory" and "information" have no "control" functions in this case. How these "primitive" forms of "memory" and "information" develop into the "control"-functional types is too difficult a question for us to answer, although obviously the emergent level of organization that is required must be multistable and perhaps even transstable. Moreover, to say that humans have memory, except as an understood elliptical expression, is a reification. The memory and information of the self-reflexive cortical subsystem are not identical with the memory and information of the system of which it is a part. The use of "I" or "the self" also involves reifications, for it identifies the organism in ways that have only limited validity: in the case of "I" the identification is often with the cortical subsystem; in the case of "the self" it is often with the general features of the human macrosystem. These reifications—apart from their embeddedness in the forms of language—imply a false epistemology of real external objects and mental representations. It is this false world view that reduces the alternatives to a unified theory of the world or an accidental world in which values are only subjective choices. If this epistemology is discarded for the one presented in this book, all specifications of "material" existences and organizations are then seen as codings that permit particular organizations of experiences in publicly communicable ways. If this is understood, the great chain of being reemerges, but not as a unilinear or total chain—as webs or hierarchies but not as *the* hierarchy. It reemerges in the realm of praxis as a world view based on consistency, "fittingness," and partial relatedness. In these more circumscribed part-relationships of the realm of praxis, meanings constantly reemerge, values are inherent in natural process, and alienation and identification are both continually transformed elements of the process.

Chapter 3

Resolution of the Analytical Problem

We have seen that a systematic analysis of the field of experience depends upon preexistent knowledge, that it includes values and so-called ordinary facts, and that statements about it are confirmed by the ordinary publicly communicable standards of science. However, with respect to questions of praxis, we are concerned with the "fit," consistency, and relatedness of the field. The way in which this "floating equilibrium" is readjusted is accounted for by other publicly communicable and scientific statements rather than by hermeneutic authentic communications. We shall now see why a global theory of social science—even if it were as restricted in its field of application as is mechanics in physics—is not available to the social scientist and how this affects matters of praxis.

Theory in Science

The great advances of theory in physical science since Galileo depended in important ways upon a choice of problems

75

permitting simple laboratory experiments that, for practical purposes, tentatively could be isolated from contaminating influences, and upon comparatively simple mathematical modeling. Neither condition holds in the social sciences, where outside influences cannot be ignored and where they are apparently not merely additive.

Unlike the Greeks, who sought solutions for perfect motions such as circles, Galileo chose a much simpler problem and therefore was on the road to success. Although we now have tools for dealing with more complicated physical problems than did the early scientists, generalization still depends upon simplification. There is, for instance, a single general formula according to which all two-body problems can be solved, given their starting positions. Attempts to solve interaction problems involving a large number of bodies require the iterated application of the formula for the two-body problem. This is an important qualification, for attempts to solve the multibody problem involve the very same simplifying assumptions concerning system parameters as in the two-body problem—for instance, frictionless motion—but nonetheless become increasingly particularized in the sense that no multibody general formula is available for application to particular instances of that category of problems. Therefore, apart from problems of measurement error or of interaction between measurer and measured object, the more complicated the problem becomes, the closer we get to a situation in which our formulations are more like the particularities of the real world than the laws that are characteristic of theoretical physical science.

Theory and Praxis

The foregoing discussion, pursued adequately, leads to the required distinction between theory and praxis. The realm of theory (and of specific propositional knowledge) is one in which axioms, theorems, and identificational codings of evidence are treated as constants for the specific purposes for which they are employed. They are bathed by the realm of knowledge, which, as explained in *Justice, Human Nature, and Political Obligation,* is in a state of floating equilibrium, the constants of which are only relatively such. This latter realm is not one of strict deduction but rather is one in which the elements are joined in terms of consistency, "fittingness," economy, and partial relatedness.

The realm of praxis accords in the area of science with one of the many, usually ambiguous, meanings attached to "paradigm" and in the area of society it accords with one of the meanings attached to "ideology" or "world view." However, these world views are not subjective or incommensurable simply because their terms and relationships are incommensurable on a one-to-one basis. For instance, the Michelson-Morley experiments on light that were so essential to relativity theory and that led to rejection of the ether were conducted within the framework of existing standards of experiment and evidence. Quantum theory, complementary theories of light, and other developments in science that changed our conception of what science is, or even of what evidence may be, developed out of an existing realm of knowledge, the revealed inconsistencies of which in some cases led to major rearrangements of the field in terms of specifics and of relationships among elements. This is an objective and scientific process even though the standards for evaluation differ in part from those used in validating specific propositions or theories.

A similar process occurs with respect to world views concerning society. The "ideology" of capitalism changes as we learn how values influence economic behavior, how financial incentives produce otherwise non-economic mergers, how the frictionless assumptions of neoclassical theory gravely distort economic reality, and so forth. One of Marx's major problems was that he was too much in the grip of a metaphysics that demanded "true" first principles. As a result, he sought a substitute for "first principles" in a class that would have an ultimately true perspective. No such ultimate true perspectives exist. There are only floating equilibria in the realm of praxis that are subject to readjustment. However, because Marx failed adequately to make the prior distinction, he failed adequately to distinguish between specific theories or propositions—based on axioms and standards of evidence that are tentatively held constant in the current "phase" of the floating equilibrium of the realm of praxis—and the world view embodied in the realm of praxis. Thus, he failed adequately to distinguish the "totality" of the realm of knowledge as it bears upon particular problems from the "totality" of a supposedly "holistic" but specific theory. These failures of distinction still pursue the sociology of knowledge. Much of the remainder of the chapter will consist of an attempt to disentangle their elements. We shall see that some of the efforts at disentanglement will move us toward particular types of world views. As we examine problems of theory application and of complementary analyses, we shall see that those that deal with broader macrofeatures of society begin to make the connections that are ordinarily thought of as world views or ideologies.

Equilibrium Analysis

Let us now see why the problems of social science do not permit even the application of a simplified generalization to different types of instances of more complicated cases. To do this, we must examine differences in the character of the equilibria that are characteristic on the whole of the physical and the social sciences. The best-known type of equilibrium is the perhaps inaptly named mechanical equilibrium. We say that a car resting on a flat surface is in mechanical equilibrium. By this we mean that the forces that might move it are canceled. These forces are not merely inferred from the resting state of the car. They can be measured independently. And their cancellation in this instance can be derived from Newton's laws. In this limited sense, all mechanical equilibria can be explained by covering laws. Although the concept of mechanical equilibrium in physics does not convey much significant information—for far more information is conveyed by the specifics of particular theories—it is more than a label; and, thus, it conveys more information than a label normally conveys.

Homeostatic systems—and, although they do not exhaust the classification, all social or political systems are variants of the homeostatic type—lack those covering laws that apply to equilibria of the mechanical type, that is, equilibria that are characterized by measurable and hence meaningful equalities. It is true that all homeostatic systems operate within boundaries set by some mechanical system: for instance, one can determine how much energy is required to raise the temperature of a room a specified number of degrees if one knows the volume of the room, the thermal qualities of the energy source, and the efficiency of the heating mechanism. However, no such independently measurable system of equalities applies to the thermostatic system. Thus, in this case, an explanation of the temperature equilibrium of the room requires reference to the way in which a thermometer operates within a system of relays designed to turn the heater on and off. In this case, "homeostatic equilibrium" is a label designating the type of system and conveys only the amount of information that a label can convey, whereas the explanation of the behavior of the system is not linked to a concept of equality. The label merely tells us that the system is one in which changes in specified elements of the system maintain one or more particular elements of the system within a "requisite" range.

This is one reason—another, and related, reason being the degree of complexity of the system—for an important distinction between theoretical analyses in the social and the physical sciences. To the extent that common terms are used in mechanics, thermodynamics, optics, and astrophysics, their measurement in experiments in each generally proceeds according to a common scale. Generally we can define and identify these terms independently of more complex system variations.

Because the units of social and political analysis do not exist in isolation, even in principle, let alone in practice, we cannot even define them in a way that employs terms for which there are common measures independent of some varying system contexts and according to which "equality" is empirically meaningful. Because this is so, we cannot develop a measure of system efficiency in processing such variables, as we can for engines that use fuels. "Demands" and "supports," for instance, do not exist in the same way as physical units, for their scale lacks a meaning that is independent of the character of the political or social system that processes them, whereas the energy contained in fuel is measurable independently of the efficiency of particular engines. For this reason, covering laws of the type available to physicists are not available to the social scientist. Statements that systems are in equilibrium when demands and supports are in balance, for instance, are vacuous for this reason.

The failure of rules or common formulations to apply across different types of homeostatic systems is sometimes misunderstood by incautious students of so-called general systems theory. They note, for instance, that the growth curves of populations within city limits and of bacteria within enclosed cultures may be similar. They then infer that general transsystem "laws" have been found.

Their mistake is that of reference. The growth curve in this case is a constant that applies to a system of population within a bounded area. To the extent that these specific properties are dominant—and this will be true only for some concrete representations of the mathematical formulas and within specified boundary conditions—the particular interpretation of the formula will provide an explanation for only some of the facets of the concrete system. It will not explain other facets of the behavior of the concrete system.

Thus, such formulas may explain certain features that some political units have in common with some non-political units, whether social or biological. They do not explain either the differences between different types of political units or those aspects of political or ethical behavior that are not relevant to those variables. They are thus not general theories but particular theories, for instance, of population growth in an enclosed area. And they function only as parameters in studies of political systems qua political systems or of bacterial systems qua biological systems. General theories cannot explain the behavior of different varieties of the same general type of substantive system. And, where they appear to do so, they will be either vacuous or consistent with contradictory applications.

Chapters 2 and 3 of *Justice, Human Nature, and Political Obligation*—in the discussions of Stephen Toulmin and of J. C. C. Smart, for instance—demonstrate how an attempt to find a general formulation for ethics turned a rule into a definition of rational behavior. The rule therefore ceased to serve as a proposition that could function within a theory. The applications of the putative rules then were shown to be vacuous. And, although the general ethical rules of John Rawls are not vacuous, we demonstrated that contradictory rules are consistent with his assumptions.

How can we then proceed in areas of investigation where this is the case? Systems analysis provides a strategy for research in such cases. Let us first examine the matter more generally. It makes sense to say that the field of knowledge, which includes all its elements, functions as a whole with respect to those of its elements that are brought to bear upon particular problems. However, analysis always requires a differentiation of the field into articulated elements. There is no mysterious, hermeneutic process that permits ordered statements about the whole in the absence of such differentiation. A related confusion is the so-called distinction between holistic and elemental approaches, where the real problem is one of an appropriate research strategy.

Whole and Part in Systems Analysis

It has been asserted that systems theorists believe—and apparently some have said—that the whole is greater than the sum of its parts. I must admit that I do not know what that sentence means, but neither do I know what "The whole equals the sum of its parts" or "The whole is less than the sum of its parts" means.

How do we add the parts of a system together? If a frog is cut into pieces, it is no longer a frog; but is it less than the sum of its parts? If we link several paper clips, the resulting chain is flexible whereas the elements of the chain are relatively rigid. The characteristics of the chain are certainly different from the characteristics of the elements considered individually, but are they greater or less? The characteristics of the chain are related to the characteristics of the parts and the style of linkage, but the characteristics of the whole and of the parts may be dissimilar; and "greater," "less," and "equal" may be quite inapt forms of comparison.

A more general form of the argument states that the systems approach is holistic, that is, that it attempts to predict the behavior of the parts from the behavior of the whole. It is quite true that the operations of a gasoline engine explain the functions of the piston. But it is also true that knowledge of pistons provides insight into the requirements of engines and of the substitutes that would be required if pistons were to be replaced. Similarly, in a perfect market, prices exist as parametric "givens" for every individual buyer and seller. But not every possible sale will be consummated at that price. What is the behavior of the whole from which individual behavior is predicted? More accurately, we would predict that no action by an individual buyer or seller would affect price noticeably in the market place. Thus, we might ignore the individual aspects of decision making in examining price (assuming, of course, that no important change occurs at the boundary of the system) but not in the autobiography of a particular seller or buyer. On the other hand, in an oligopolistic market, we might need to know the conditions of the individual sellers to predict price equilibrium.

Yet, even to the extent that these strange words, "Predict the behavior of the parts from the behavior of the whole" or "Predict the behavior of the whole from the behavior of the parts," have any meaning at all, it is clear that their meaning depends upon the type of system we examine. In a perfect market, we pay less attention to the individuating features of buyers and sellers. In an imperfect market, we must pay more attention. In all cases, we must know which aspects of the boundaries of the system, if they change, will in turn change the motivations of the buyers and sellers either individually or in the mass. We must also know through which type of system these behaviors will be filtered, for the impact of the behavior will depend upon the type of systemic filter. Thus, some business systems tend to eliminate "cutthroat" competitors and others to encourage them and to eliminate ethical businessmen.

Even to the extent that the conceptions have meaning, to argue that systems analysis chooses holistic over elemental methods of analysis fundamentally misconceives the systems methodology. The systems approach does not say that knowledge of individual actors is largely irrelevant in predicting behavior; it says that predictions concerning certain classes of behavior must take into account the systemic relationships of the actors. The extent to which one requires information about an individual or system depends upon the characteristics of the system, of the actors, and of the environment in the particular case that is to be examined. This cannot be predetermined on the basis of general principles.

Theory and Application

Part of the confusion over the relationship of whole to part may result from the fact that theories are not designed directly to predict particular results. Thus, for instance, Newton's laws do not mention the sun or the earth. All particularities are ignored. However, to predict when an eclipse will occur, specific information about particular bodies must be fitted into the general equations.

Theories of economics, for instance, do not include within their formulations particular transactions. Thus, some students of social science may think that when dealing with such systems the particular is determined by the system. But what happens instead is that when the particularities of the individual case are stated, their use within the general formulation permits, to the extent that the theory is sufficiently precise, a prediction that can be verified.

Yet one does not need to know much of economics to know that a farmer who suffers from ten straight years of drought is likely to go bankrupt. In this case, the prediction is made empirically on the basis of specific information without any resort to more general theories of economics. All that this shows is that the suit must be cut to the cloth. These matters are not governed by general principles or by engaging debates between scientific schools but by the requirements of the particular cases. An economist who attempted to explain the shutting down of a business by a sole proprietor whose only son had died by reference to abstruse economic theory would be recognized as stupid. So would an engineer who thought that the laws of physics had been proved invalid when the engine of his car failed to start in the morning. And an inventor who explained that his perpetual motion machine failed because one of the parts was rusty would also be stupid.

Whether an explanation is offered in terms of systems of interaction or in terms of actors depends upon circumstances. For instance, a manager of a baseball team may explain that he had a runner attempt to steal second base in the late innings because he needed one run to tie the game. This explanation is offered in terms of the strategy of the game. It pays little attention to the particularities of the individual players, although it does refer to the circumstances of the individual game. In another case, however, the manager may explain that the pitcher was taking a long windup and that the catcher had a bad arm, thus making the steal a percentage play. This explanation rests almost, but not entirely, upon the particularities of the actors or players. Which explanation is more or less appropriate depends upon the conditions of the case and the question that is being put.

For instance, if one wants to explain why banks lend money, the answer is to earn interest. If one asks why a particular loan is made by a particular officer of a bank, the answer may lie in the credit characteristics of the borrower, in his personal relationship to the lending officer, or in the attempt by the officer to establish a record for loan acquisitions. These two levels of explanation are different but related. For instance, if one inquires into the reasons why a bank became unprofitable and went into receivership, the answer may be, for instance, that too many officers made loans to friends who were bad credit risks in order to embellish their lending records. However, even "deviant" behavior acquires meaning only in terms of role expectations within a system. If we do not know how banking systems operate, and that lending money in certain ways is a regular function, we do not know why a particular act of lending is deviant. On the other hand, we cannot explain the deviance except by bringing into account particular features of the situation that the more general account of banking ignores.

Similarly, despite Habermas's belief to the contrary, role theory can be applied to an account of change. His mistake arises from that fact that he is familiar with role analysis only in the examination of a single system in a more complex system. Considered from an interactive standpoint role analysis can help to account for change.

Actors are embedded in social and political systems in such complex ways that role conflicts often arise for them. Thus, an actor often must choose which set of role norms he will fulfill and which he will neglect or disobey. Moreover, because the actor can detach himself from any particular social system in which he is a participant, he must be motivated to act in ways consistent with its critical limits; and the other actors must be motivated to induce him so to act if the system is to persist.

The actors are embedded in a web of systems. Thus John Jones has both nuclear and extended family relationships, a role in the business in which he is employed, a social and recreational role, and perhaps a religious role, among many others. For some sets of environmental circumstances these roles may be not merely consistent but irreconcilable. Thus if Jones is a teller at a bank and if his wife desperately needs an operation and if he can get the money in no other way, he may have to choose between robbing the bank at the expense of his role as teller or failing his wife at this critical juncture. If Jones fails his wife, his family situation may be destabilized. It is unlikely that the failure of one clerk would destabilize the banking system. However, revolutions occur when critical numbers of key individuals respond to the demands of other role functions at the expense of their role functions in the state system. The conflicts that arise in cases of this kind are, along with the environmental changes that stimulate the problem, among the causes of social change. This kind of cross-sectional problem can best be studied by examining how, under various types of environmental conditions, critical roles in different systems make critically inconsistent demands upon the critical actors who participate in the relevant set of systems. This is but another form of applied systems analysis or of engineering systems to the real world or of praxis. This helps us to understand why social change is virtually necessary if society is complex and the environment varied. Because social changes produce at least some major dislocations, they also will produce alienation, as will be seen in part 2.

This also helps us to understand the dispute between determinate structuralists—we ignore the unfalsifiable hypotheses of the deep structuralists—and existentialists. No choice can be made in the absence of a structure, whether of the personality system, a social institution, society, or culture. However, which is dominant in determining choice depends on circumstances and framework of reference. In a perfect market, the market equilibrium is dominant in determining price. Nonetheless some producers may choose not to sell at that price. Monopolies may determine the price/output ratio they desire subject only to certain inelasticities in the market or political constraints. A small elite (or an important individual) may dominate a large social system in which case its (his) demands will determine much of the behavior of the large system. Because individuals perceive the self and its requirements in terms of the framework of understanding of the time, culture, if not a social institution, will dominate individual choice. Yet, because conflicts of choice occur within cultures, transstable personalities (a term that will be clarified in chapter 6) reinterpret the culture in making some choices. In this case, a cultural transformation occurs that could not be predicted from the culture and other elements of the environment alone, without taking into account the judgmental capabilities of the transstable personality and the coding system with which it receives and responds to the acculturation process. Thus, neither structuralism nor existentialism as an exclusive mode of analysis is adequate in accounting for this process—any more than is Habermas's neo-Kantianism.

"Objectified" Wholes and Intersubjective Consensus

Because social behavior requires the pragmatic use of concepts, it is sometimes asserted that institutions are objectifications of an intersubjective consensus. This terminology either misapplies the concept of intersubjective consensus or it vulgarizes Hegel's concept of objectification.

Hegel was an objective idealist. In his philosophy, all existents—whether men, social institutions, or nature—were objectifications of Mind. However, particular men, institutions, and natures were not objectifications of concepts or images in the minds of particular men. Hegel definitely was not a subjective idealist.

To use a contemporary mode of expression, social behavior is impossible in the absence of minds in some sense, even for animals. All behavior is mediated by reasoning and/or coding of the perceptual system. However, the beliefs men have concerning social institutions may be different, and perhaps even discordant, without instability provided that they permit sufficient complementarity of behavior.

Thus, intersubjective consensus, as that term is often used, is not a requirement for the existence of society. Moreover, institutions may, and usually do, dominate the thinking and acculturation of men. They possess a reality that cannot be reduced to the beliefs of men, whether intersubjective or not.

If talking about society requires the existence of thinking people, so does talking about particular men, or values, or qualities such as color, duration, or hardness. Such discussion always makes use of an object language. That is, concepts are used that refer to objects of thoughts. In this sense, the ontological status of social institutions, men, machines, trees, values, and qualities, for example, is similar.

To the extent that concepts such as objective and subjective are useful, discussions of "wholes," including society, or of particulars refer to objective features of the world. Society is not an intersubjective phenomenon, let alone a matter of intersubjective consensus, even though its existence requires some complementarity, if not necessarily concordance, of mind "sets."

From particular analytical perspectives, particular macro-features of a society often can be treated as "givens," while other features, depending upon historical particularities, may vary within limits without necessarily being better or worse. The features that are variable from particular perspectives are called societally idiosyncratic features, although no particular distinction between "givens" and variables has absolute (or exclusive) ontological status. These variable elements fall within, although they do not exhaust, the category of what others improperly call intersubjective consensus.

Complementary Frameworks of Analysis

Many questions of concern to social scientists do not lend themselves to a single or unitary framework of analysis. To illustrate this, we will first start with a case similar to that usually found in the physical sciences: the adjustment of a single framework of analysis for the initial conditions of application. If President Truman, for instance, had wanted to know whether an atomic bomb would destroy Hiroshima, the engineering theory of the bomb would have provided an answer to the question for him if some "if" clauses had been filled in, such as the bomb's being correctly constructed, being loaded on the plane, arriving at its destination, and being dropped on target. If, on the other hand, the same methodology is applied to President Kennedy's behavior during the Cuban missile crisis, it is unlikely to work. Let me illustrate why. In the former example, there is a single central theoretical logic that could be applied, if initial conditions are given. In the latter case, we have a number of cogent logics. A strategist might have argued that Kennedy would likely have acted as he did if the United States had conventional and nuclear superiority. A student of international relations might have argued that he would act strongly if he were afraid that a failure to do so would produce some other crises elsewhere, for instance, in Berlin. A student of domestic politics might have argued that he would have acted strongly if he wished to win the election. And a student of psychology might have argued that he would back down to test the principle of unilateral concessions. Each of these conclusions is based upon a theory sketch. There is no way that these theories can be combined together in a single deductive system. And each of these theories has some validity in general and with respect to the predicted or to-be-explained properties. Although it is possible that an obsessive president might take into account only the variables of one of these theories, that is highly unlikely. They are not conflicting theories. Even if in principle they might give rise to different conclusions, they express complementary logics that the mind may apply simultaneously to the same event—or at least to the same relevant properties of the event—in some judgmental fashion. In *On Historical and Political Knowing,* I suggested a principle of "restricted choice": "In deciding that choice is restricted in particular ways, we often have no good framework within which accurate weights can be assigned to particular perspectives or within which *ad hoc* relationships among them can be well articulated. Even the process of identification of a particular aspect of an event or of a series of events with the framework chosen to illuminate part of it is an identification based upon criteria subject to question." This is merely a special, but easier-to-understand, case of the general discussion in that book of the fact that initial conditions in social science predictions are derived from a variety of theory sketches and not simply estimated directly as in the physical sciences.

In applied theory, theory is engineered for specified boundary conditions. In the Cuban missile crisis case, a series of complementary theoretical sketches or perspectives are applied. The essentially deductive reasoning within each theoretical sketch is explanatory. The choice of relevant theory sketches and the assessment of their contribution to the outcome is within the loose equilibrium of the realm of praxis. In that realm assessments are made according to considerations of consistency and "fit."

How an observation is coded—that is, the determination of what elements of observations are "identified" as evidence and what they are regarded as evidence for—depends upon many other elements of the field of knowledge. The transition from Newtonian to Einsteinian mechanics, although involving differences in the concept of mass, substantially retained the older categories of evidence. Yet even within the realm of physics some observations are disregarded as inaccurate because they do not "fit" contemporary theory. The mitogenetic ray was an example of a case in which theory-conforming observations were made that were later discounted as inaccurate.

Sufficiently great shifts in the theoretical structure of science may produce great changes in the coding and interpretation of evidence. Except in the twilight zone, however, this does not mean that competing theories cannot be compared "objectively," for the weight of the field of knowledge likely will "validate" the new coding, particularly if, as is likely to be the case, some of the old codings sustain the new theories that require altered codings with respect to other evidence. Thus, it is the revealed inconsistency in the old field of knowledge that shifts the entire field. The pioneer in science, the great theorist, is one who intuitively "sees" the discrepancy earlier and who recognizes first the new mode of integrating the field or at least of restoring substantial consistency to it. However, there is no global theory that accounts for physical reality. There is only a shifting equilibrium in the realm of praxis, including a multitude of theories and of standards of evidence.

Marxian Theory and Complementary Frameworks

Our earlier example of the Cuban missile crisis illustrated the problem of praxis at the microlevel of analysis, that is, at the level of individuals as actors. Marxian "theory" attempts to develop social theory at the macrolevel. Because, however, Marxian theory aspires to a theory of history, it employs a global logic that attempts to unite different logics from different areas of social science. Because the frameworks respond to different foci of analysis, because they cannot be compressed together or derived from a fundamental theory, and because their boundary conditions cannot be uniformly stated, they cannot be part of the single theoretical system that Marx apparently attempted to supply. In history, consistency and "fit" are the key variables. Objective reasons can be offered for conclusions concerning either interpretations of the past or prescriptions for the future. But interpretations are never "gapless" and social solutions in complex systems never fill all needs.

As my own theories of international relations pertain to the macrolevel of analysis, I shall use one of them to analyze briefly how a theory at the macrolevel may be applied to the real world and why Marxian analysis fails in this respect.

A major question is whether a theory sketch, that is, a loosely universalistic system of "laws," accounts economically for the evidence—whether it fits. A particular theory may "fit" some real-world situations but not others. This matter is not *merely* descriptive, however. For instance, with respect to my "balance of power" theory, the theory does not seem to describe the properties of events in Europe after 1871. The reasons for this are specified below. We would expect that in a "balance of power" system alliances would be short-lived, based on immediate interests, and neglectful of existing or previous alliance status. The rigid alliance systems of the European great nations between 1871 and 1914 and the relatively unlimited nature of World War I would seem, superficially at least, inconsistent with the prescriptions of the "balance of power" theory. We could, of course, resolve the problem by analyzing the period from 1871 to 1914 in terms of a rigid "balance of power" system.

This solution, however, would require us to analyze every characteristically different state of the world in terms of a different systems model, thus depriving the concept of system of much of its theoretical utility and turning it into a primarily descriptive device. The alternative procedure is to decide whether the underlying theory of the "balance of power" system can be used to explain the observed discrepancies.

We do not, of course, assert that if the theory of the "balance of power" system can account for the behavioral differences from 1871 to 1914, it therefore is *the* true explanation of the observations of system properties. Undoubtedly, other factors played important roles in producing both the specific properties of the sequence of events and the properties of the general form that the sequence took. We will merely have established that the asserted irregular properties do not invalidate—or are consistent with—the theory and that the theory may be useful for relating a wider range of observations than is possible in its absence. This may increase the confidence we place in the theory and its explanatory power.

The reconciliation of theory and observed properties follows. If we recognize, as there is reason to believe Bismarck foresaw, that the seizure of Alsace-Lorraine by Prussia led to a public opinion in France that was ineluctably revanchist, this parameter change permits engineering the theory in a way consistent with the developments that followed. As long as Germany was unwilling to return Alsace-Lorraine to France, France would be Germany's enemy. Thus, France and Germany became the poles of rigid, opposed alliances, as neither would enter—or at least remain in—the same coalition, regardless of other specific common interests. The chief motivation for limitation of war in the theoretical system is the need to maintain the existence of other essential actors as potential future allies. For the foreseeable future, however, neither France nor Germany was the potential ally of the other. Consequently, neither had an incentive—as would normally be the case in a "balance of power" system—to limit its war aims against the other. What had been an incentive for limitation became instead a disincentive. A somewhat analogous problem occurred with respect to the alignment pattern of the Italian city-state system. In this system, Florence, for a considerable period of time, functioned as the hub of opposed alignments. In the case of this system, the explanation involved a geographic factor.

These engineering examples need to be distinguished from the ordinary ad hoc use of hypotheses. As in the case of physics, which posits how bodies behave in a vacuum, my "balance of power" theory sketch examines how an international system will behave if states optimize external security. Both posits are counterfactual. Nonetheless, it is possible to utilize such theories to explain what will happen under specific but different circumstances. In the case of the European "balance" after 1871, it can be established independently that French public opinion interfered in particular and definite ways with the optimization of French external security. If these specific "starting states" of the system are engineered into the theory sketch, our predictions would be consistent with the actual behavior of the system. The difficulty is that we have not a complete theory but a theory sketch, that the boundary conditions and the required confirming evidence are not completely stated, and that therefore the level of confidence in the explanation is low. The theory sketch, however, is consistent with what did occur and, everything else being equal, what happened is what one would have expected on the basis of the theory.

Moreover, these theory sketches can be falsified in principle and sometimes in practice. Thus, it can be shown that my "balance of power" theory correctly describes behavior during appropriate portions of the classic Greek city-state system. However, the explanation provided by the theory is wrong. It can be shown by independent evidence that logistic (and some political) reasons played a far greater role than strategic reasons in the maintenance of the equilibrium of the system. On the other hand, independent evidence can be adduced to show when the Italian city-states began to behave in accordance with the theory sketch for the reasons the theory would indicate. (This occurred during the period of Lorenzo in Florence.) Thus, such theory sketches, although soft in a scientific sense, do come within the ambit of empirical science.

As many readers may know, I employ different types of theory sketches to explain international systems for which the "balance of power" theory sketch does not have explanatory power. Suppose that we interpret Marx's use of "class," "forces of production," and "relations of production" as categorization. We might then argue that they merely specify the types of variables to be employed in Marxian analysis; and we might then treat Marx's theories of feudalism and capitalism as separate and comparative theories of economic systems.

Even if we were to do this, a number of serious problems would remain. Although Marx often seems to use "inevitable" as a statement that applies within the framework of a theory rather than as a real-world prediction, he never clearly specifies which variables are part of the theory sketch and which are parameter estimations that are employed in an effort to assess its relevance for a real-world situation. In short, there is no adequate delineation between the statements of his theory sketch and of his application of the theory sketch to the real world. Thus, there is ipso facto no articulated statement of the parameter conditions that produce the dynamic evolution of his model and those that might produce a different outcome. That is the primary reason why Althuser's use of "overdetermination" becomes truistic.

If Marx had ever made a systematic set of statements, even apart from other difficulties of his model, he probably would have had to specify different evolutionary paths for economic systems under different real-world environmental conditions. As he states his theory, there is a constant pressure to reduce the world to the theory, that is, to a unilinear pattern that is fundamentally uninfluenced by the rest of real-world conditions.

Finally, we come to a brief analysis of the internal problems of Marx's formulations. If profit can be made only from the surplus exploited from labor, it follows that profits should be highest in those industries with the greatest proportional concentration of labor. This is the mechanism in Marxian theory by means of which the growth of capitalism produces a decline in the rate of profit which then drives the capitalist toward the exploitation of external, and more primitive, markets.

However, by the time Marx was writing the third volume of *Capital*, he discovered that those industries with large proportional concentrations of capital made more profit than those with large proportional concentrations of labor. Marx therefore argued that he was talking about the average rate of profit in the entire system and not the particular rate of profit in any company. Yet if profit is exploitation, then the exploitation must be greatest where the profits are highest.

Presumably, if the Marxian argument in the third volume of *Capital* has any validity, it would mean that the more industrialized the society, the lower the rate of profit in it. That is not borne out by experience, unless Marx would now argue, if he were alive, that he is talking about the world as a whole, whatever that may mean.

Obviously the Marxian labor theory of value breaks down. Moreover, none of Marx's empirical research serves as more than an illustration for the rather vague, although intellectually interesting, logic of the argument employed in *Capital*. The theory cannot be reconciled with any other theory and it cannot be reconciled with itself. Its conclusions are in obvious conflict with an enormous amount of evidence. The vast profits available to Europe, Japan, and the United States for capital investment coexist with high wage scales. They bear little, if any, relationship to trade with, or "exploitation" of, underdeveloped areas.

Some writers, such as Paul Sweezy, agree that frozen labor in the form of technology may invalidate Marx's law of falling profit; but they claim that they find "contradictions" between capitalism's search for profit, its production processes, and the "real needs" of man. However, this mode of argument attempts to maintain Marx's conclusions at the expense of his theory. Even so, it raises more questions than it is capable of answering. Does the increased profit come only from "frozen labor"—a formulation that begs the question with respect to the prior labor and entrepreneurial skill of the entrepreneurial class—or from current entrepreneurial skill? Perhaps Professor Sweezey should examine what happens when capital is available in areas that lack entrepreneurial skill. Moreover, what is a "real need" and how do we relate it to Marx's arguments? We have shown in chapter 1 the essential fallacy in such arguments.

Marx's "solution" appeared to work even poorly only because of his failure to make a systematic analysis of the part systems within his argument: a failure that was "justified" by his claim that such analysis would "distort" reality—an objection that is invalid, as we have seen in the discussion of holistic and elemental analyses earlier in this chapter. Despite Marx's recognition of differences between European and Asian feudalism and of the possibility of different developmental paths to socialism, he never fully overcame the belief that his theory was general: in short, that it was a theory of history that applied to all societies and their histories. Differences in development merely represented differences in adaptions to different circumstances. Socialism, despite these differences, was "inevitable," at least short of catastrophe.

Marx's basic error lay in the concept of totality. With Hegel, he distinguished between particular knowledge that is partly true and partly false and knowledge within the totality in which inner relations are "really" true. This error was far more understandable in Hegel's idealistic philosophy where it imposes a coherence upon the world that collapses the distinction between mental operations (even if only within the *Geist*) and reality. In the idealistic version of this theory, concepts have their true place within a universally valid hierarchical system, even if it cannot become known to the finite minds of actual human beings. This type of coherence theory of truth presents reality as a cosmically sophisticated and multidimensional jigsaw puzzle. However, it divorces Divine knowledge from human knowledge in such a way that we cannot proceed from the human to the Divine. No criteria exist to show to what extent, or in what respects, existential "coherence" is a "true" rather than a "false" coherence.

Although Marx's system is not as "neat" as Hegel's, many of the same implications are subsumed in his concepts of "totality" and "inner relations." If the discordant elements of reality could be brought into direct and eufunctional relationship, it might seem that things would lose their "objectification" and would be related directly to a system of internal relations in which each element has its "natural" place in a totality. Marx's analysis thus assumes some variation of a coherence theory of truth.

The distinction—not absolute, of course—that we make between theory and praxis avoids this disabling result. Although the criteria for knowledge are different in theory and praxis, both types of knowledge arise out of man's interaction with other men and with nature. No assumptions are made about the "coherence" of the world. Instead, in the realm of praxis, statements are made about the compatibility of theories, propositions, and observations concerning delimited portions of the world. In the realm of theory, confirmations are made of deductions from theories the assumptions and interpretations of which can be treated as "givens" because they have a high consistency within the realm of praxis.

Praxis, in this view, is not coherent in any grand sense. The theories and the interpretations that are regarded as consistent have a "tight" fit only at the "center" of the field. Even so, concepts, axiomatic structures, and assumed parameters do not have one-to-one relationships. Nor will they join neatly at the boundaries. There will be overlaps of subject matter and different ways of investigating similar phenomena, depending upon research purposes.

Theories accord with each other when their styles, assumptions, and modes of analysis "fit together" or "relate partially." More specific characterizations of metaphoric concepts such as "fit" require concrete analysis in particular cases, as when we examine the "fit" between particular chemical and physical theories. In some instances, the "fit" may be very close, as in that between physics and chemistry, although not so close that one can be deduced from the other. In other cases, such as that of physics, biology, and physiology, the "fit" will be much looser and will depend upon particularities that are even more loosely related: for instance, the fact that earthly physiologies are based on carbon and oxygen rather than silicon and methane. The looser the relationship, the more accidental it becomes from a metatheoretical standpoint.

That all part systems (or theories) are related to at least some other part systems (or theories)—to a greater or lesser extent—does not imply a univocal set of ordered relationships for all part systems even in principle. To speak of a totality in this sort of situation is to misrepresent the degree of relationship between elements of the realm of inquiry. This mistake metaphorically replicates the mistake of the analytical/synthetic dichotomy, for it assumes a system with nothing outside of it. However, as shown in *Justice, Human Nature, and Political Obligation,* the methods of both praxis and theory are closed. Both methods are partial. Both attempt to find congruence. Both require information from outside their closed "deductive" and "assessment" techniques, information produced by man's interaction with the world. And they do so much more extensively than is true of analytical systems. But the world is open, while the methods of science are closed. Therefore thought cannot be used to communicate about the world as a whole.

Let us recapitulate this important conclusion from a related perspective. When a mathematician says that one transfinite set is larger than another, an esoteric—and, from a practical point of view, peculiar—use of language is employed. It is true that for any finite number, the set of integers is larger than the set of even numbers. However, for the same number of operations—that is, enumeration of numbers—each set will contain the same number of numbers. And each set "exists" in only a peculiar definitional realm.

Nature does not provide a univocal ordering of its parts. Hegel's Absolute was a complex idealistic version of such a univocally ordered "total" set. If one were to treat Hegel's terms literally rather than in the dictionary sense—for instance, "opposed to," or more literally "standing against," rather than "object" for *Gegenstand*—this might not be the case. In the latter event, Hegel's Absolute might be a process rather than a thing. In this case, the Absolute, his concept of infinity, and his theory of quantity might be related conceptually; and he would have anticipated, metaphorically at least, Georg Cantor's concept of transfinite numbers. Even then, Identity would not genuinely characterize the Absolute, for although the elements of every numerical sequence would parallel elements in some other numerical sequence, every sequence would also be different from every other sequence in some characteristic. And there would be no supraset in which all cohered, although there would be a class or set to which they belonged: the set of transfinite numbers.

Although Fichte's insistence on German as an *Ursprache,* the writings of the brothers Grimm, and Schelling's naturalism might seem to justify an *ur*-interpretation of Hegel's language, I know of no professional philosopher who accepts it. In any event, this interpretation will do the Marxian conception of alienation no good, for Hegel's Absolute in either case is outside of History in a way that Marxian

Communism cannot be outside history. Time and physical existence would also be absent in the Hegelian Absolute. In real time, in which Marxian Communism is to function, "contradiction," or at least conflict, necessarily is always present.

At least, however, transfinite sets are produced by specifiable operations. If "totality" is thought of as the limit of operations that can be applied to the multidimensional world, we really do not know even as much as we do in the case of transfinite sets what is being proposed. And the use of "existence" is even more peculiar. Moreover, this concept of totality plays no useful role in inquiry and—except for the hint that we will never exhaust meaning or, alternatively, that all assertions are to be understood from within the framework of the realm of knowledge (either of the individual or of the society)—carries connotations that are quite misleading and that would be avoided by more descriptive phrases. The more we move from metatheory to theoretical applications, as in Marxian theory, the worse the misrepresentation becomes.

In the application of theories, particularly but not exclusively in the social sciences, the fit will be much looser than in metatheoretical statements; and the "fittingness" of deductions from a variety of theoretical frameworks—as in the Cuban missile case—may differ from case to case. Thus, the frameworks that account for the variance in the Cuban missile case may differ, at least in part, from those that account for the Bay of Pigs decision. It was the attempt to collapse such elements—and the concept of totality—that produced the uneliminable discordance between Marx's theory of history and his examination of particular histories. Epistemologically, we always enter in the "middle" of the story. There is no true beginning and end. All knowledge is relative to the manner of inquiry.

Our view shares with the Marxian the belief that the world is known in the concrete as man interacts with it (transfinitely, in my terms) to make of it something that accords with his nature, the existential (dispositional) aspects of which are also transformed in the process. However, to speak of "essence," "thing in (or even for) itself," or "the structure of reality" is to hypostasize this process. A process is a reality. It is not *the* reality. And, although the transformation of existence, including concepts and methods, by human action, including inquiry, is a concrete "reality" process, it is not asymptotic, except possibly with respect to selected aspects of reality. Nor does it guarantee a "unity" of knowledge, as contrasted with relatedness.

I prefer the term "world view." The world is not a totality in the Marxian sense. "World view" responds to the concepts that are valuable in Marxian thought by treating them metatheoretically. A world view consists of the more general features of the realm of knowledge. The relationships between separated clusters of the pattern may be infinitesimal.

Connectedness enriches theory and praxis. And theory and praxis may explain and assess connectedness. But neither, nor both together, can guarantee "total" connectedness or important connectedness in a totality. Those concepts remains idealistically metaphysical in the pejorative sense of the phrase even within a philosophy that is ostensibly materialistic.

Marx's failure ultimately lay in his failure consistently to understand that no part of the field of knowledge—or of an encapsulated social world view—can be insulated from the equilibrial process of the field. There are no absolute constants; and revisions at the periphery of the field ultimately affect the center. This is precisely what so many Marxian theorists religiously attempt to avoid.

Meaning

In the test in principle, I developed an iterative procedure that is applied within an interactive framework of knowledge and that permits men to make statements about the social world that are not simply the products of their social positions. In the distinction between first- and second-order frameworks of values, I showed that no entirely common framework for value statements exists. However, the identifications of men with other men and with institutions produces at least a partial first-order framework. And the test in principle establishes a common second-order framework. Let us now examine the problem of empirical meaning to see how other problems posed by the sociology of knowledge can be resolved.

It is meaningful to say that we could predict Soviet policy if we sat in on meetings of the Politburo, although we have no way of doing this. It is meaningful to say that knowledge of our strategic superiority in 1962 led the USSR to retreat during the Cuban missile crisis, although we have no practicable way of proving this and may not even have a ground for preferring it to alternative hypotheses. There are tests in principle for distinguishing such alternate hypotheses. In these cases we know how to make the test, but have only limited access to the required information. In other cases, a method may not be available to make the test. The Greeks did not possess the mathematics Galileo required; but his problem was always meaningful, although it was not always known to be such. Newtonian mechanics depended upon the invention of the infinitesimal calculus. Nonetheless it was scientifically and empirically meaningful to talk about physical mechanics before the invention of the infinitesimal calculus.

Something is meaningful if we can state the experiments or canons of evidence that in principle at least would permit its evaluation. An example of a meaningless hypothesis would be one that argued that particular entities determine the behavior of subatomic particles but that permitted no independent test even in principle either for directly discovering such entities or for inferring their existence from the behavior of subatomic particles. No possible observation could invalidate such a hypothesis and it is consequently meaningless.

Where the subject is too complex for actual experimentation, distinctions can still be made between types of systems. For instance, if a fair coin is thrown into the air, one knows that over the long run, each side will appear with a probability approaching 0.5. The operations of a roulette table are more complicated but can also be specified. If a strong man tosses a chair high into the air in a tumbling pattern, we cannot specify the spot on which the chair will come down, the particular path in the air of the chair, or even a reliable probability statement about the latter. We can, however, state certain likely characteristics of the motion of the chair in the air and give reasons for this. We can also discuss certain differences between the behavior of the chair and the behavior of the coin and perhaps derive certain consequences from these differences.

Essentially this is what we have done with our preceding discussion of human systems. Although we know very little about the internal workings of the human system, we can specify certain definite differences between it and other types of systems and make reasoned hypotheses about certain broad aspects of its behavior for which we have some direct and some indirect evidence. Moreover, this evidence, even if weak, is essential to our attempt to understand the human system. We cannot understand human behavior if we do not understand the existence of information-distorting psychological mechanisms within the human personality or the reasons for their operations.

This is a rather general problem. We cannot understand the behavior of a banker unless we have some understanding of the banking system within which that behavior functions. It is not true that we understand the international behavior of the United States when we say that a person with a particular name carries out a certain international action. Knowledge that a man with that name is president of the United States is essential to our understanding of the action. This is not a reification but an essential element of the information required to understand the action.

The Sociology of Knowledge

There is a second element of Marxian theory that gave rise to the sociology of knowledge and that carries over into the argument about whether objective knowledge is possible. This suffers from the same defect as the more general form of the argument concerning objective knowledge. The assertion that class determines social perception either is determined by one's own class position or it isn't. If it is determined by one's class position, then it has no status as an objective truth. If, on the other hand, it is not determined by one's class position, it can be confirmed independently by a social science observer, regardless of social class. If this is the case, either the assertion is self-contradictory or a narrower assertion is intended.

The narrower assertion might be that people tend to perceive the social world from the perspective of their class position. Thus, the laborer may see his wages as low and his ability to support his family as poor. The capitalist may perceive the profits of the company as resulting largely from his managerial expertise and the search for profits as requiring low wages. The laborer may call the employer exploitative, but this will be meaningless unless he can show that some special circumstances provide the employer with a monopoly over his labor. Otherwise, he means only that he may prefer a system that distributes wealth differently. Even here, he may not be able to show how this is possible economically or without hurting others; in any event, we are now in the realm of ethical discourse. However, both the employer and the employee may be able to understand both why the other perceives the situation as he does and the interests supported by these perceptions. In this narrower form, the proposition asserts that people tend to perceive the world in ways that are consistent with their interests and values. Thus, at the very least, we can achieve second-order objectivity with respect to their assertions and the conditions under which they are produced.

Studies of administrative tribunals tend to show that in contested cases judges with upper-class backgrounds tend to believe testimony by managerial employees, while those with labor backgrounds tend to accept the evidence adduced by working-class witnesses. Except to a naive person, this is surely not surprising. What would be surprising would be the inability of the arbitrators ever to perceive any evidence as rebutting the testimony of those they tend to believe. The problem here necessitates a distinction between the objectivity of knowledge, the availability of evidence, and the recalcitrance of many individuals to assess the evidence fair-mindedly.

Where, for instance, testimony conflicts and the relevant independent evidence is scarce, most judges will tend to accept the evidence presented by those individuals in whom, for whatever reason, they have the greatest confidence. Confidence in testimony may rest upon appearance, demeanor, a common framework of values, or a community of interest. Testimony about evidence may be in conflict and independent standards for the evidence may be difficult to acquire.

It is possible to specify various objective methods of determining the existence of different types of bias as well as to devise tests in principle that determine what actually happens. For instance, well-constructed survey material may show the existence of various types of bias in class-related perceptions. These materials may not indicate what environmental conditions produced these particular types of differences of perception or these particular classes of identifications, particularly if the surveys were based upon narrowly defined environments. On the other hand, comparative evidence may be of assistance here.

In addition, events can quickly be play-acted before groups of individuals. Their differences in perceiving the staged events can be analyzed systematically. Thematic apperception tests can be given to different groups of people and social differences in interpretation can be analyzed. Other tests can be used to disclose the extent to which a teacher's perception—based, for instance, on previous communications of the IQs of people represented in pictures—will be communicated subliminally to students.

With respect to the staged events, we know what happened because we have the participants' testimony as to the planning that went into it. The material that arbitral tribunals go over is not determinable in the same way. However, we can specify a test in principle. Much of what "really happened" is what would be shown by tapes taken from properly located TV monitors. These would reveal the actual course of events. They would not make completely evident motivation or perception. However, we have tests that could elicit information about these elements, although not with high confidence. These would include lie detectors, Freudian analysis, and testimony given while under the influence of truth serum. Apart from other inherent limitations, their use would be limited by our ability to understand the appropriate questions that need to be asked, but this is true even when we are questioning nature.

Where these texts exist in principle, there are methods in principle for determining the truth, although they may not be available in practice. These give philosophical meaning to the concept of objective truth. In actual practice, our methods may provide such low confidence in the results that we prefer some specifiable distribution of biases on arbitral tribunals. Even this evaluation, however, rests upon a propositional evaluation that is putatively objectively true.

The Nomothetic—Ideographic Controversy

According to those who take the nomothetic position, social science must use universal terms for qualities as do the physical sciences. This is the route to the study of "lawful" behavior according to the nomothetic position. Those who take the ideographic side of the controversy believe that the social sciences deal with particulars, and that specific descriptions of places and of actors are essential to understandings.

It can easily be seen that both positions point to real aspects of the problem of analysis and that both misunderstand real aspects of it. To convey information about a particular to another individual, we must always abstract and generalize it. Thus, green does not exist independently in the world although particular objects may be perceived as green. Generalization, as an abstraction from a particular, links it to other examples of the same thing; in this sense generalization makes a universal.

If the ideographic is literally taken as the particular, then the position is self-contradictory, for any finite description immediately involves universals and never exhausts the particularity of any entity. If, however, the ideographic is regarded as referring to those universal aspects of being that are hypothesized on the basis of relatively direct sense-linked, qualitative knowledge, it may refer to the more commonsensical or natural types of description: to color, heat, and pressure, as contrasted with such second-order or scientific concepts as mass, energy, and gravity. In this variant of the ideographic position, those types of universal concepts are rejected that acquire their meaning within the framework of theoretical systems.

There may be a still different orientation from the standpoint of which the ideographic implies the particular. Although all descriptors involve universals, the greater the number of descriptors that are applied to an entity, the more it is particularized in the sense of being distinguished from any other existential entity. Thus, by employing a sufficient number of descriptors we would enable someone to identify a man as a particular man rather than merely as a member of the class of men or of the class of Americans. If we discuss a man's behavior, we discuss those elements of his history and experience that distinguish him from other men. However, can we explain his behavior without some reference, either explicit or implicit, to nomothetic concepts? This is unlikely if by nomothetic we mean only related to a theory rather than literally according to a law. It may be a fact that Richard Nixon was president of the United States. However, to understand the actions of President Nixon it was not sufficient to say that Richard Nixon did something, for the things he did as president could have been properly understood only within the framework of the American constitutional system. Even if the expected consequences of presidential action do not occur, an explanation of this would employ specific data within the framework of the appropriate system of explanation, for instance, his having provoked a constitutional crisis.

When a physicist applies nomothetic concepts to experiments, the experimental conditions usually are controlled exhaustively; the experimental behavior, therefore, is determined by the variables under study. Because such terms as "heat," "energy," and so forth, are independently measurable, their meanings are usually directly applicable to diverse physical systems. Independent measures do not exist for the generalizations exployed in homeostatic systems; and all social systems are variants of the homeostatic type. Therefore, attempts to use key variable terms such as "demand," "nation," "ruler," "mother," and so forth as if their meanings were the same in different types of social systems usually produce a level of abstraction that reduces the level of information and that often consists only of vacuous generalization. This leads to the illusion that social science is an ideographic science that uses particular names. This illusion is reinforced by the fact that we are usually interested in applied experiments or explanations in the social sciences in which the specific environmental conditions of the problem are essential to analysis. However, this very same problem arises if we try to explain, for instance, why a particular physical experiment failed or why the engine of an automobile did not start on a particular day.

Therefore, the application of nomothetic concepts in social science runs into specifiable difficulties for which comparative analysis is a partial answer. In any event, we cannot adequately explain human or social behavior without the use of nomothetic concepts. On the other hand, our practical interest in the results of historical "experiments" usually makes "identity" problems of central concern—a type of concern that, for practical purposes, is foreign to the student of microphysics although it is not entirely irrelevant to the student of astrophysics.

Furthermore, the realm of history is the realm of praxis *par excellence*. It is the world in which consistency, "fittingness," and the analysis of partial relationships permit a closed, and therefore incomplete, reconstruction of the texture of a period or of an episode in history. Thus, the ideographic position is misleading, for it does not take account of the fact that theory and explanation do apply to particular aspects or sectors of the realm of knowledge. On the other hand, the nomothetic position is misleading because it misdirects attention from the particular nature of existential being—a factor of far more concern in the social and political world than in science—and of the role of assessment in relating the elements of the realm of praxis.

Conclusions

The route of this chapter has been long and circuitous, but it has outlined a metamethod of empirical investigation that deals adequately with normative judgments and matters of praxis, and that also dispenses with the mystical core of Marxian dóctrine. The concept of alienation loses its ideological status. Alienation is no longer a global problem requiring a global solution, although it may be recurrent and to some extent ever-present. Alienation is a practical problem that requires different practical solutions at different times.

As in the case of all practical problems, inadequacy of knowledge, differences in types of alienation and in the seriousness of each, the availability of adequate means of response, and genuine disjunctions of interests lead us toward solutions the relevancy and adequacy of which differ according to time and place. Reduced from the level of theology, where it ranks with original sin in the discussions of learned conferences of Catholic and Marxian theologians, alienation is a problem to be solved in practice by real men with real needs—men who work, love, and compete or cooperate in real environments and, under adverse conditions, against real dangers.

Part 2

ANALYSIS

Chapter 4

Alienation

Alienation and Socialism

Much of the moral power behind the idea of socialism lies in the concept of alienation. The ideas of socialism and of alienation are powerfully joined in the writings of Karl Marx. The system of capitalism, including the market economy that constitutes its foundation, treats labor as an ordinary commodity. According to Marx, the process by which the market sets the value of commodities becomes a fetish in capitalism. Under capitalism man is alienated from his human nature. Although his labor upon natural objects (plus the "frozen labor" in capital goods) produces the value of the finished goods, he does not receive this value. Instead his labor is bought and sold according to its commodity value.

Thus, the capitalist receives a surplus value that has been exploited from the laborer. Those who own capital have a class interest in continuing this form of exploitation. Thus, capitalism, because it organizes human beings into classes, which are defined by their relationship to the means of production, produces antagonistic conflicts of interest between men. In this sense, the game of alienation is played out under capitalism in the ghostly form of class struggle. Man can escape alienation, and its consequent false consciousness, according to Marx only by transforming capitalism into socialism.

I shall not repeat my criticisms of the labor theory of value upon which much of Marx's argument rests. However, its inadequacies have produced intellectual difficulties in socialist countries which have discovered the economic necessity of placing an economic value upon all inputs that go into the productive process and not only upon labor. It has driven them to logic-defying circumlocutions in explaining conflicts of interest. The so-called non-antagonistic conflicts of interest by means of which socialist countries explain conflicts they no longer can ignore are called non-antagonistic by fiat: only conflicts related to class differences based on the formal Marxian definition of ownership can be antagonistic. By Marxian fiat, differences arising from social location or authority relationships unrelated to formal "ownership" cannot be antagonistic. This body of doctrine is merely a modern form of scholasticism that obscures societal and economic analysis. Despite the empirical richness of Marx's analysis, his most general concepts, including alienation, are never related adequately to his empirical materials. Therefore, they are abstract in even his sense of that word.

However, even the most detailed demolition of the Marxian arguments would be largely irrelevant from a practical point of view. Many people feel alienated and this feeling will impel them to search for some solution that promises an escape from it. During some of the sit-ins in the universities, a number of students were heard to say that they felt alive for the first time in their lives. They felt that they had overcome alienation and were leading authentic lives. If the forms of violent demonstration have diminished, this does not necessarily mean that alienation has been overcome either in fact or in belief. It may signify only that many have accepted their inability to change what they perceive as an alienating process. They may still distinguish between a system that alienates and one that overcomes alienation.

Marx did not discover the concept of alienation or even, more specifically, alienation under capitalistic conditions. The first modern economist, Adam Smith, pointed out the alienating characteristics of modern industry. Unlike the artisan, the factory worker may work on a task as trivial as making the head of a pin. His fragment of the task is so remotely related to the work of the factory that it alienates him from the meaning of work, which thereafter becomes merely a means for earning money. Hegel developed a more systematic view of alienation and explored how the dialectical process alienated man from nature, from society, and from work.

The Meaning of Alienation

We have no interest in exploring the history of the use of the concept of alienation. The meaning of the concept, however, does concern us. The way I shall use "alienation" is more neutral with respect to the conclusions I shall draw than is usually the case in radical writings. The set of terms— "alienation," "identity," "creativity," "authenticity," "productivity"—employed in this book will enable us to deal with the subject of alienation within a reasonably comprehensive and adequate framework.

The dictionary tells us that the alien is the foreign. If this is the meaning that is chosen, a man who is alienated would be in some sense foreign or separated from himself. In this case, do we refer to his feeling different from what he was previously or different from what he thinks he ought to be? Is he a stranger in his own society—one who does not belong? Is an alienated person abnormal? Would this imply that he differs from other people in this respect? Can an entire society be alienated? Would that imply that the society differs from others in this respect? Or from what it ought to or could be? How would we recognize a person who was not alienated or a society that did not produce alienation?

Obviously, ordinary usage leaves us with many problems. In one sense we might seem to be dealing with a verbal paradox. How could one be alien from oneself? Is it not true that one is identical with oneself and, therefore, not alienated? One could be alienated from one's work or from one's country but not from oneself. But perhaps this gives us a key to understanding the term. Alienation occurs when an individual perceives an absence of meaningful relationships between his status, his identifications, his social relationships, his style of life, and his work. As such situations often arise, alienation is a recurrent phenomenon.

All complex systems that are subjected to significant environmental disturbance, or that have important needs whose joint satisfaction cannot be managed within inappreciable time spans, become dysfunctional in some respects as capacity is drained to deal with disturbances or specific needs. In self-conscious systems with a sense of identification and life style, such draining of capacity produces alienation, that is, dissociation in the meaningfulness of the life of the individual. Part of one's life appears to be both "objectified" and "detached" from the rest of it: it appears to respond to external constraints rather than to personal desires or needs.

Yet the process is more general than this suggests, for living necessarily "objectifies" the various aspects of existence—that is, it gives them a form or content that often escapes control as circumstances change. This loss of control is experienced as a disjunction between the self and important aspects of the world. Thus, alienation is always potential in the human condition.

Differentiation

The first time that a man considered what he would do in the future, he treated himself as an object of his own thought.

The first time that a man named himself, he differentiated himself from other people and from the fullness of his being. The first time that a man classified himself as human, he differentiated himself from other animals, from nature, and from inanimate reality. Life involves a continual process of differentiation.

When we think about a problem, we interfere with, or cut off, that part of reality that would be conveyed by a direct emotional response. On the other hand, if we allow ourselves to respond with emotional intuition, we have cut ourselves off, to that extent, from the information that abstract thought could present about the matter. When we think about ourselves or others, the categories of thought we use, the language we employ, the theoretical concepts we develop open up certain insights and cut off others.

To think of ourselves as human is to overlook our continuity with the animal kingdom. To think of ourselves as animal is to diminish the moral and intellectual capabilities that our biological organization provides. To think of ourselves as Americans diminishes our kinship with the rest of mankind. To think of ourselves as part of mankind diminishes our contribution to the institutions that maintain important human values in the United States.

Differentiation and Alienation

Some differentiations are so great that even the absence of a meaningful relationship is not perceived as an alienation. A female pig that is perceived by a male pig as an object of sexual attraction, for instance, is perceived by a plantation owner either as a source of income or as a potential plateful of ham. The average person does not think of himself as sexually alienated from pigs, even if they are of the opposite sex, for he does not perceive a potential identification.

Clearly, "alienation" and "differentiation" are related terms, for the former cannot occur in the absence of the latter. Clearly, "difference" and "distance," if only as meta-phors, are required for alienation. The extent of "distance" or "difference" that is necessary to produce alienation is the core of the problem.

Therefore, if the extent of "distance" is the key variable, the potential for alienation is omnipresent. Yet not every distinction or separation produces an actual alienation. There is an obvious sense in which the farmer is "alienated" from an aspect of the pig that is essential to the pig's nature. However, it is unlikely that this "alienation" alienates the farmer from an important aspect of his nature.

The primary source of alienation lies in the discrepancy between the identifications of people in actual societies and the satisfaction of their needs or desires in social activities. When the identifications of the individual appear to be sub-ject to social or natural forces over which he has no control, he perceives himself as alienated from important aspects of his personality. Such alienations occur often if the society fails to produce what humans perceive as satisfactions of legitimate human goals. It occurs as social change disturbs identifications in ways threatening to the personality of some members of the society; for example, women's liberation in contemporary society becomes a threat to some male identi-fications. Equally, however, the failure to achieve it becomes a threat to new female identifications that are perceived as legitimate. It occurs almost inevitably in complex societies because of conflicts between at least partly independent part-system needs. These can never be entirely reconciled. Thus, disorder and lack of symmetry are inherent in the human condition.

Marx's Solution

Marx was aware that alienation was related to differentia-tion, although he surely did not confuse the terms. He was aware that social processes produced alienation by thrusting men into activities that divorced essential aspects of their humanity and that separated them from nature. We have seen that the sociological or class analysis on the basis of which Marx arrived at his conclusion is unsound. But perhaps a few words should be said about the philosophical presuppositions that led Marx to expect such a conclusion to be valid. The concepts of internal relations and totality that Marx took over from Hegel constitute the key. Although we have treated this matter at greater length in chapter 3, we note here that Marx's solution is substantially, if not completely, harmonistic, for it assumes that no antagonistic conflicts will exist between part systems of the larger social system under socialism. In all complex systems, in which scarce resources must be used to obtain more than one independent variable or social outcome, simultaneous maximization is impossible in principle. The greater the complexity of the system, the more likely it is depending on scarcities, that conflict between independent goals will increase strain in the system. In the absence of adequate feedback and favorable environments, the more likely it is that the system of relationships will push to a limit and be transformed. This is occurring to capitalism, although its transformation to socialism is far from obvious and appears to be so in Marxian theory only because of Marx's inadequate account of the sociology of capitalist society. But this process in principle is eternal.

Alienation and Existential Being

Alienation is an inevitable, although not an omnipresent, component of existential being. If one worker is alienated because his wages are set by the market and because his livelihood may disappear during an economic storm, another worker may be alienated because his diligently worked and beautiful product gets no special recognition. It may be true that recognition is not necessarily monetary, but there is a constant tension between rewarding a man for being who he is and rewarding him for what he does. Either choice devalues some aspect of him, denies its relevance, and separates him from it. Such choices are always so costly to some men that these men are alienated.

In the real world scarce resources often require choices concerning the fulfillment of desires in cases in which the attainment of one desideratum is not directly linked to the attainment of the others. Yet it would be intolerable if the strength of the desire behind a motive continued unabated in consciousness until satisfaction occurred. Usually without thinking about it, the conscious aspect of desire is suppressed until it can be satisfied. Nagging signals may rise to the level of consciousness, but the strength of the motive is usually rerouted to an area "below" consciousness. It is in another (alien) place, ready to be resurrected upon an appropriate signal. If circumstances forbid its satisfaction, it is denied, suppressed, transformed, or mitigated by some form of secondary gain; in these latter cases, alienation is present. Sometimes the suppression becomes relatively permanent. An aspect of being, rather than being temporarily delayed until an appropriate time, is "outlawed," and secondary gratifications are substituted for it. Such individuals lack authenticity—a subject to which we will return in later chapters.

There is a routing system within the biological system. Certain types of signals are suppressed, delayed, transformed, diminished, intensified, and so on. Information is compartmentalized, transmitted, suppressed, and used. There is a complicated "economic" balance in the system. The maintenance needs of the subsystems of biological man are not identical with general system needs or each others'; and often there is considerable conflict. There are barriers and thresholds within the system. It is not instantly permeable from an internal perspective any more than from an external perspective. And, as we know, the internal subsystems even play tricks on one another, as when an undesired thought or feeling rises to consciousness or an unanticipated word is spoken.

The very singleness of being we present to others, and to ourselves as well, is in part the product of control by that cortical subsystem that dominates consciousness and that, in some of us, tries to outlaw or alienate other aspects of our being. In some sick individuals, it gets its "comeuppance" in the form of hallucinations or of other disturbances produced by other subsystems that have broken through the suppressing mechanisms of the cortical subsystem. Are these antagonistic or non-antagonistic contradictions? Or should we eschew such obscure terms and recognize that opposition is as ineluctable an aspect of life as symmetry and cooperation and that, if this is the case, some expressions of it will produce alienation?

Some antagonisms arise from the fact that the environment is limited. The individual who has a heart attack while running away from danger could have avoided that attack if the danger had been eliminated. Two individuals on a boat with enough food for one would not have been faced with this problem if sufficient food were available. On the other hand, two individuals who wish to head a particular organization are in inevitable conflict. Although this particular conflict could be removed by providing an organization for each, honor, esteem, and other similar values are inherently comparative. These conflicts can be avoided only by changing motivation. But then esteem will be extended to those who efface themselves or who avoid competition. And esteem always has a comparative element. Nature can never be sufficiently bountiful to accommodate all ambitions, for comparative evaluations defeat such a condition. And those ambitions or values that are sufficiently denied will produce alienation.

The Illusion of Eliminating Alienation

The cases dealing with the limitations of nature give rise to the illusion that all could be harmonious if only nature were sufficiently bountiful. The cases dealing with the esteem awarded men give rise to the illusion that all could be harmonious if only there were a new man who was not motivated by envy, greed, or the need for esteem or honor. Essentially, alienation is to be eliminated through productivity, changes in social organization that eliminate competitiveness, and changes in the motivation or consciousness of men that eliminate competitive or egoistic desires.

Unfortunately, this process of reasoning involves a sleight-of-hand trick. Each particular focal point of alienation or "contradiction" is removed by rearranging some other elements of the system. Because each type of alienation can be removed in imagination, it is imagined falsely that all of them can be removed simultaneously. This is impossible for biological man, let alone for man in society.

Internally, the sophisticated human biology requires adaptation of part system to part system. As in the case of every other type of circuitry, system compromises are required. Moreover, in this case, there are a number of system compromises that have not been designed by skilled engineers but that have resulted from the processes of biological evolution. The physical organization of the brain involves the layering of new functions over older and more primitive ones rather than a completely redesigned unit optimized for the requirements of biological humans.

The illusory character of a claim to eliminate all forms of alienation becomes even more understandable and explicit when we move to the level of social organization. Will the society of the future require surgeons or physicists? These skills require training. Training is costly in terms of time and requires sacrifice. Time spent studying skeletal structure cannot be spent at museums, listening to great music, or engaging in any number of delightful activities. During this time, the psychological mechanism of denial is required to reduce the import of these losses. Rationalization is required to enhance secondary gains. Secondary gains might well include such things as recognition, which has value primarily in terms of ambition.

Human society requires police forces, garbage squads, industrial organization, legislative activities, judicial functioning, and so forth. These functions can be performed only if the organizations that perform them survive and if they are serviced by individuals who perform the functions that maintain organizations. Yet the survival function of an organization can never be synonymous with the survival of the society of which it is part. This introduces a necessary conflict of interest between an organization and the system of which it is a part.

An organization requires people to carry out its functions, and this requires that the people who are supposed to do this be motivated actually to do it. Yet their needs are never synonymous with the needs of the organization, and therefore there is an inevitable conflict of interest between them and the organization. Thus, on the average, people tend to rise in organizations if they are skilled in survival techniques. What is good for the survival and rise of officials within an organization is not necessarily good for the organization, although partial conflicts of interest need not be total. When these conflicts are great enough—and in complex systems, some will always be that great—alienation occurs.

The Universal, the Particular, and Alienation

Justice requires rules. Yet every rule is a general statement that abstracts from the particulars of a situation. In principle, justice should take into account all the particularities of a situation. In the absence of rules, no one could be assured that the relevant particularities would be considered. Yet, in complex systems, some rule applications will be incompatible with substantive justice. This is one of the sources of some of the problems discussed in chapter 4 of *Justice, Human Nature, and Political Obligation,* and it produces alienation.

Freedom, Necessity, and Alienation

The freedom of a stone to roll is dependent upon a spherical shape. The freedom of a person to think is dependent upon certain types of biological organization. Action requires some particular kind of structure. Thought requires some particular form of symbolism.

Particularity is ineluctably a limitation. And limitation always involves some form of separation. The stone would not roll if it were not separate from the surface. The mind could not engage in thought unless it were at least partly independent of other aspects of the body. Thought could not occur unless words or symbols were differentiated from each other. If everything were infinitely transformable at will, we could not think, for we could not make reliable projections into the future. We could not act, for we would have no experience on the basis of which to calculate the consequences of our own actions.

The object upon which we work could not be used by us if it did not have predictable characteristics. Those very predictable characteristics make it at least partly independent of our will. The language we employ in the process of thought could not be used publicly by us unless the meanings of words were independent of our individual wills. Yet these necessary characteristics become dysfunctional in some circumstances. Words cannot change their meanings fast or often enough for all uses. Language too, like all tools, can produce alienation.

It is the concept of alienation in the general sense that is a fetish, for it separates us from the nature of the problem. By positing the elimination of alienation, it holds out the dream of an alienation-free society. In effect, it promises a perfect disturbance-reducing control system that will eliminate all important conflicts. Yet, even in the narrower sense of economic alienation, its Marxian use is a fetish. Apart from his faulty method of defining social classes, Marx never offered a specific explanation of how socialism would remedy the particular defects he found in capitalism and, especially, the alienation of man as a consequence of commodity fetishism. It was not enough to establish how this alienation occurred under capitalism. It was required that he analyze how a socialist form of productivity would change this fact. In fact, alienation is abundant in those socialist systems that have removed the market mechanism for determining value. The extent of absenteeism and sabotage in socialist economies provides striking evidence for this assertion. Moreover, welfare capitalism has modified, and in the future may minimize or eliminate, the absolute dependence of the worker on his market value. (Chapter 7 will carry on this discussion in a different context.)

The Marxian Error and Dysfunctions in Communism

It is the separation of Marxian theory from analysis of the real world—in effect, the reification of theory—that tends to drive successful Communist revolution into one of two forms of dysfunction, the extent of which depends on particular conditions. Insofar as every form of organization designed to achieve Communism in the revolutionary state must develop vested interests of its own in order to survive, it therefore must oppose itself in part at least to the most general goals of the Communist state.

It also responds to the individual interests of its own executives. Consequently, the regime may be driven into a frenzy of suppression. Society may be torn apart, organizations uprooted, and the forces of resistance fragmented in order to eliminate those "heretical" tendencies that are inconsistent with the new society. Because the forces of resistance reach down to the individual level, family life and individual autonomy may be suppressed. The lives of men are regimented and politicized, for otherwise they would sink back into the old forms of humanity. Because the end result that is to be achieved is ontologically impossible, no particular form of social organization or manifestation of human personality can satisfy it.

In its extreme manifestation every element of independence and of difference becomes evidence of the continuation of counterrevolutionary alienation. The closest comrades in arms, the most trusted confidants, the most distinguished philosophers of the revolution ultimately reveal their counterrevolutionary tendencies. As the Maoist Han Suyin sympathetically expresses it in the *New York Times* of 29 August 1972:

> At all times revolution demands choice, choice between self and dedication. To the day of his death, no revolutionary can be sure of not erring, for always the enemy within the gates lurks, and that is no other than the self, clamorous with its own personal demands; lust and ambition and pride. Liu saw himself the head of an elite mandarinate. Lin plotted a military coup.

In the extreme variant of this condition, the most insignificant differences in doctrine or the smallest deviations from state policy become symptoms of these counterrevolutionary tendencies, for, obviously, if alienation had been eliminated and if harmony reigned, these differences would not exist. To a limited extent this is why some of the early Bolsheviks were able to confess to "objective" counterrevolutionary tendencies, for their subjective dissent from the conduct of the regime entailed the ultimate disloyalty: recognition not of a minor or of a trivial failure in the revolution but of an essential failure. Yet, if the goal were possible and if it needed to be achieved through the party, then even the subjective assertion of failure is counterrevolutionary. If the revolutionary goal is impossible, then their lives are meaningless. If the goal is possible but betrayed by those who hold power, then their silence and acquiescence constitutes the ultimate betrayal of their beliefs. Yet, if they are not silent, the regime will crush them. Denial, repression, projection—the gamut of the psychic mechanisms—are all required to attempt to cope with the crescendo of disturbing information.

An endless effort to eliminate alienation would be extremely costly. It would debilitate the military forces of the government, interfere with economic reconstruction, undermine the orderly administration of activities, and threaten chaos. Yet ordinary activities require effective administration. Railroads, airplanes, and tractors need to be built. Individuals need to be trained to accomplish these tasks. Mail has to be collected and delivered. The wilder the revolutionary frenzy, the greater the need for order.

Eventually revolutionary frenzy wears itself out, even as the requirement for purity within the revolutionary movement continues to lead to schism after schism. While the revolution turns on its own children in the effort to eliminate alienation, the forces of resistance gather in the normal institutions of society. This leads to the second alternative *modus operandi* of the revolutionary regime: that of survival. Alienation is accepted and suppressive activities are turned against those who threaten the maintenance of the regime. Ideological purity, although not conformity, is downgraded. The prime requisite is to maintain the authority of the current holders of power and to suppress challenges to them.

Thus, Communist regimes tend to move from extreme radicalism to extreme conservatism. Order, hierarchy, and authority become the latter-day keynotes of the regime. Change, other than technological or quantitative, is viewed as threatening. Economic improvement is designed to reduce discontent and to immobilize the desire for change. The original ideology is now used primarily as a pacifier: for, if the public can be made to believe the class theory of revolution and if classes have officially disappeared, no further revolution is possible. Political dissent can then be treated as a psychological aberration, for the possibility of reform that it suggests is delusional.

The restoration of capitalism is threatening not because the regime fears the restoration of alienation—the conservative Communist state multiplies alienation—but because it threatens the rationalization of the regime's power. The disagreement over the reintroduction of market methods then becomes a clash between those who see this as a means for improving economic pacification and those who see the market mechanism as a potential disturbance of the political equilibrium of the regime. Thus, the Communist regime must protect its ideology with the same tenacity that a neurotic uses to protect his neurosis. It is the crutch it uses to walk through life. Even if the regime cannot sprint with it, at least it is mobile. And the threat is real enough. Removal of the crutch would remove the rationale of a regime that can be defended on no other ground, for the divine, the democratic, and the technocratic rationales have been dispensed with.

The Leninist conception of morality according to which all moral rules become subordinate to revolutionary goals is subject to most of the problems that attend the dysfunctions of "true autonomy" that will be discussed in the next chapter. Socialist goals are largely undefined; the relations between actions and consequences are highly overdetermined in a complex world; and the evaluation of intermediate goals and of their relationships to more distant goals is complex and ambiguous. As a consequence, behavior becomes dysfunctional for reasons adduced in the next chapter.

Maoism attempts to avoid the bureaucratic conservatism of Russian Communism by continual irruptions from below. Apart' from the defects produced by Mao's inadequate conception of social structure and alienation, this process cannot survive the charismatic personality that protects it and is almost certain eventually to produce a rigid bureaucratic repressive countermechanism. In the interim it disrupts the lives of those who suffer its effects and subjects their actions and even their thoughts to external, and thus alien, controls.

Chapter 5

Ontological Dysfunctions
of Mind

If alienation is an ontological necessity in a complex world—
and I have argued that it is—the attempt to eliminate alienation
will generate instabilities. Although particular alienations can
be overcome, it is inherently impossible to eliminate alienation.
These attempts to escape alienation may produce loss of
identity, madness, and frenzy. I do not pretend to give a
complete account of these phenomena, to deny that their
course is affected by interactions with other social, biological,
or mental processes, or to claim that they are produced only by
the attempt to eliminate alienation. However, I do propose that
there are relationships between the attempt to eliminate
alienation and the dysfunctions of mind—perhaps not in
every case, but in a sufficient number of cases to make the
interrelationships of the concepts illuminating.

The Compulsive Dysfunction

In the compulsive form of dysfunction the mind attempts
to unite reality with subjective belief by making them iden-

tical. Thus the compulsive person fits external events into a constricted set of highly ordered categories. He has a strong, although impoverished, sense of who he is and a weak sense of his relationship to the world. The magic acts performed by the compulsive—stepping on cracks in the streets, making symbolic movements with the hands—have the meaning of restoring the ordered relationship between the perception of self and the perception of the world. The reality that does not conform is brought back into relationship by a magical gesture. In effect, alienation is overcome by psychic denial. This individual has a sense of identity that is continually buttressed by distorted perceptions of the world and by magical forms of control over it.

The compulsive is also an obsessive. Because the symbol is the instrument by means of which the external reality is reduced to the mental conception, the symbolic means of achieving this is a requirement—obsession—of the individual's state of psychic adjustment. As these obsessive means are the instruments of control, the sense of identity, although real, is fragile; it is constantly subject to assault because of the inadequacy of the magical means of control. The compulsive (obsessive) individual is alienated from his own emotions, because these are threatening to the psychic order he is attempting to impose upon the world.

Disorder continually threatens to break through the defenses of the obsessive-compulsive individual and must be guarded against rigidly. This requires strong magic. The magic pentagram, designed to contain the summoned devil, is a good example of this aspect of the compulsive's behavior. Its sharply angled lines, its rigid forms, and its perfect circles are particularly appropriate to the portended victory of form over spirit. Yet the pentagram is designed not to exclude spirit, but to control it, to contain it within the accepted forms. It thus seeks to overcome the alienation between the two by harmonizing them, by excluding the obnoxious, autonomous, intellectually uncontrollable aspects of emotional life. What it fears is the free play of spirit, the unbridled emotion that reveals its distinctness from form and from intellectual control. The Freudian may explain this syndrome differently, perhaps by referring to fear of punishment by the mother of sexual expression by the child. This explanation also may be valid; the factors employed in the two modes of explanation are not exclusive.

I am not arguing that biological or libidinal drives and mind are inherently incompatible but only that they are different and not entirely adaptable. Whatever the reason for the origin of the fear of the independence of impulse, the meaning of compulsive magic lies in the assertion of the complete harmonization of mind and emotion. That such an extreme effort to overcome it emphasizes alienation is not paradoxical. The patient who refuses to recognize the sickness of his condition often worsens it. It is precisely the attempt to escape all alienation, as in the case of revolutionary Communist movements, that intensifies it.

The compulsive person is not anomic. He has a set of rules, but they do not provide him with directions that are sufficiently responsive to the richness of the external world. His actions are stereotyped; they are not productive.

The Sociopathic Dysfunction

The second form of dysfunction—essentially the sociopathic—is represented by the attempt to overcome all alienation by a plasticity of individual adaptation. Some sociopathic people present those faces to the external world that meet the requirements of particular situations regardless of their continuity with past behavior or their conformity with reasonable sets of rules for social intercourse.

This dysfunction may take a variety of forms including that of the true sociopath, who simply uses other people, and the essentially rudderless individual who is merely searching for approval. In the extreme case, this leads to loss of identity. The individual does not know who he is because he bends his behavior to the inconsistent requirements of a constantly shifting set of external pressures. The only constant in his behavior is inconstancy. He is incapable even of perceiving his character as changed, for there is no consistent pattern from which it changes. This person merely seeks to survive, or perhaps to prosper. He is an embodiment of the Hobbesian axioms which—rather than expressing true premises about the nature of man—rationalize the aberrations of dysfunctional character. Again, as in the case of compulsive behavior, this aberrational pattern is defended for the secondary gains it provides. However, the quest is both hopeless and costly, for the adaptations of the anomic person who lacks a robust sense of identity are inherently incapable of satisfying the demands that are made upon him by his personality. Thus, the sense of alienation gathers strength.

Dysfunctions of Sensitivity

Some of the forms through which the attempt to escape all alienation is pursued produce madness. The attempt to reduce the barrier between the individual and the external world in some cases leads to a heightened sensitivity that escapes control. Pater's imagined sensorium—an organ emitting different odors—is representative of the effort made by the decadents during the *Yellow Book* period in England. Attempt after attempt is made to heighten sensation, to distinguish different forms of sensation, and to exhaust that mode of experience. In its extreme form, this process becomes autonomous, escaping conscious control and severing the relationships between the individual and the everyday world. As external experience is unable to produce the range of experience the individual now requires, he turns to a world of imagination. The elements of this imaginative, kaleidoscopic process lose their ordered relationships. The most rapid changes of form, meaning, and appearance assault perception. The individual becomes the passive spectator of his own inner experience, merging with it almost as the clay merges with the intentions of the sculptor.

This form of aberration requires the most rigorous defense mechanisms against the intrusion of conscious control or interference by the environment. Even when induced by drugs, it is possible that the dependency of the individual is not so much upon the biological effects of the drug as upon the subjective impression of oneness with the world. However, this oneness is achieved at a price. Beyond the giving up of relationships with, and control over, the external world, the individual submits to the autonomy of the elements of subjective experience. He buys this oneness by attempting to lose himself within it. Yet this can never be achieved: for, if it were achieved, the experiences would belong not to him but to the individual elements of his experience, in which he merely appears to lose himself.

It is this ultimate incompatibility that drives the sequence into an ever descending spiral. Once the individual is caught in its power, each stage requires a further stage, for the inherent dichotomy in the experience defeats the unity that is sought. Always one appears to be on the threshold of the ultimate experience that will break through the barriers of being to produce a marvelous oneness in which no alienation occurs. Yet ultimately each new sequence of experience disappoints.

The price is enormous. By submission, the individual has given up those means of control that would enable him to interpret and understand the experiences he is having. The words and concepts his thought employs, and the logic he uses, cease to have determinate meaning. His subjective lucidity is an illusion. Through shifts of meaning, through the equation of incompatibles, through the derivation of illogical conclusions from premises, through the perception of different forms of illusory samenesses, the critical faculties of mind have been killed. The lucidity that has been achieved is the lucidity of the idiot. "Yes" equals "no," and the elementary distinction that is required for one bit of information according to the axioms of information theory has been lost.

The dysfunction of sensitivity may take another form—an excessive sensitivity to the subjectivity of other beings. We are familiar in everyday life with simple differences in sensitivity. The difference between eufunctional and dysfunctional sensitivity is often a matter of degree and circumstance. Some extreme psychopaths are willing to do anything to anyone, provided it is costless to them. Some recognize the needs only of their own families. Others have sensitivities that extend to the needs of their countrymen. Some men give some consideration to all of mankind. Some are kind to animals but not to insects. Some are kind to their dogs but will eat meat. Others are offended by the eating of animals. In extreme pathological cases, some may view the eating of plant life as a form of cannibalism. In this last case, a complete equation is made among all forms of life. In principle, perhaps, this pathological sensitivity may be extended to all of existence.

This extreme sensitivity constitutes another method for attempting to overcome alienation. It identifies the self with all the elements of the rest of the world. Ultimately this quest is impossible for obvious reasons. The refusal to eat anything would soon result in death. However, depending upon the conditions with which the world confronts us, even much milder forms of extended sensitivity produce dilemmas that can lead to madness. Sometimes we must kill or watch others being killed. Sometimes we must see our family in pain or produce pain in others. We are continually confronted with situations in which we must produce pain—a pain we may feel empathetically but never directly.

Under ordinary circumstances, we solve these problems by various psychological mechanisms that depress our sensitivity, or that divert information, or that produce rationalization. In the person of exquisite sensitivity, however, these particular forms of self-protection are no longer available. His life becomes anguished. His attempts to avoid conflicts of this type become ever more exquisitely extended.

Each extension of his sensitivity, although designed to reduce the alienation between him and the rest of the world, increases the alienation. As the sensitivity to injury increases, no matter how great the empathetic subjective distress, the sense of ultimate disjunction between self and other is heightened. The sensitive consciousness is acutely aware that the real sufferer is an "other." To escape this distress, the sensitivity is heightened still further, thus again heightening the self-punishment and the subjective sense of alienation. If the earlier type of sensitivity represents a retreat to internal subjectivity (the perceptual level), the latter type of sensitivity is relevant to the religious spirit. It is pain and the body that must be escaped.

Both these forms of escape mechanism have their obversion. The individual who intuits the dangers of excessive inner experience, but who is susceptible to the need for such experience, may attempt to avoid it through rigid mental control. The individual who is excessively sensitive to the pain of others may attempt to escape through one of a variety of mechanisms. He may attempt to isolate himself from the world, or he may do deliberate injury as a form of denial, or he may attempt to attach others to himself as a way of denying their separateness. Or, alternatively, in some individuals sensitivity, rather than being genuine, may serve as a denial mechanism. It is designed to inhibit fear of external punishment for these attempts to obliterate the distinctions between self and the external world. This extreme fear of loss of control is related to an infantile drive for omnipotence.

The Dysfunction of "True" Autonomy

There is a third mechanism by means of which the individual may attempt to overcome alienation. In its extreme form, it will produce madness. This is an attempt to overcome alienation by breaking through what is perceived as the rigid structure of social or moral rules. Individuals who attempt this escape perceive the rules of society as artificial barriers to their desires, and, hence, to their "true" or authentic autonomy. Rules about neatness and cleanliness are seen as restrictions on natural behavior. Rules about theft, particularly theft from large corporations, are seen as artificial restrictions on the needs of poor people or free spirits. Rules against incest are seen as artificial restrictions on the varieties of love. Such rules individually and collectively are seen as barriers to spontaneity of behavior.

The "free" mind perceives such rules as alienating the self from inner being. Such minds see themselves as superior, for they believe they have seen through the fakery and artificiality of society. Such views are tempting, for many rules can be violated in the individual case without any significant harm. A single theft from the supermarket is a petty matter. Moreover, some rules, even within the same society, could be supplanted by some different rule without significant harm in the long run of cases. By rising to the "superior" point of view that rules are, therefore, arbitrary, the individual appears to have penetrated to an ultimate truth. Other individuals are seen as merely creatures of habit who follow rules blindly and without understanding because of training and propaganda.

However, this attitude increases rather than decreases alienation (and anomie), for it detaches the individual from his orientation to the world. Lacking guideposts and standards of comparison, the individual case becomes even more difficult to judge than ordinarily. There is an infinity of rules to choose from in determining what is best.

Because we are dependent upon consistencies and continuities in life—we do not wish to analyze each cup of coffee for poison, or fear that a kind word will elicit a blow, or that today's friend will arbitrarily become tomorrow's enemy—the "free" spirit comes into constant collision with the requirements of his own existence. To maintain his posture, he is continually driven to further extremes. The world he seeks to unite to him eludes him. The necessity to force fate increases as do the demands he must make upon life and his associates.

As the intimate associates and followers of this free mind require some guideposts for their own behavior, he must play god, and provide such rules; and they must submit. Yet, in the absence of external standards, the standards he provides must be arbitrary, and they are changeable. Therefore, they can be accepted only as a manifestation of his power. As there is no external standard by means of which this power can be satisfied and as submission by followers may merely cloak the seeds of eventual disobedience, the leader must keep testing his power. Nothing can suffice to suppress doubt entirely. Thus, the fear of alienation keeps rising and his personality becomes fragmented. If any pattern or logic remains to his behavior, it is necessarily an internal pattern or logic that is disconnected from the external world and therefore alienated from it.

There is no solution for this case, for each further activity only increases the sense of alienation from the real world. Each act makes the individual and his group ever more peculiar and likely ever more destructive, for recalcitrant reality somehow must be brought back into connection with the self. The disconnection between the world and the self becomes so great that only destruction momentarily provides meaning by temporarily bringing the individual back into connection with the external recalcitrant world. By stamping out the disorder (disagreement with him) in the external world, he has assimilated it to himself and "proved" that he is real.

Biology and Dysfunction

If the category of alienation is an ontological necessity, it does not follow that every case of alienation is an existential necessity. Mention has been made of the fact that the human biological structure is the culmination of a series of mutations (accidents). The evolution of man did not entail the evolution of a completely new neurological structure that was fully adapted to his new being. Instead, new structures were added to the old, as in the case of the cortex and the medulla oblongata. As in the case of every other system involving complex feedback relationships, the potential for instability and overload is present in such a complex system. We know very little about the complex structure of the brain, but evolutionary advantage did not likely produce a brain that is as efficiently and eufunctional as possible. Even if its operation is far more marvelous than anything we can now conceive of from a theoretical point of view—even if it is far beyond our power of comprehension and understanding— there is room for enormous mischief in its actual operation under particular conditions. Moreover, even the best-designed system can be overloaded, in which case instabilities occur. The human brain is not likely a "best-designed" system; and there are genetic variations in the system among individuals as well as differences in its care, nurturing, and "education."

Thus, the brain can be put into dysfunctional operation by biological defects, chemical inputs, electrical discharges, libidinal inputs, and informational inputs. Moreover, there can be an extremely complex relationship among these elements. For instance, a chemical strain upon the system may lower the threshold for a libidinal or informational strain and vice versa. This might operate in terms of step functions, each new level of which might stabilize, even if not optimally, or it might produce a progressively unstable series of step changes. In the abstract little can be said about this. Few audio engineers would be willing to make predictions about amplifier circuits unless they could study these in detail; and, of course, amplifier circuits, complex as they may seem to the layman, are idiotically simple in comparison with the human neurological circuitry.

There are many competing explanations of mental breakdown: psychological, biological, chemical, organizational, and ontological, for instance, among others. Sigmund Freud speculated that every neurotic or psychotic disturbance had some biological foundation. Freudian and chemical explanations of psychoses may be inconsistent only from an extremely narrow point of view. Exclusive attributions of cause and effect may do more to obscure than to clarify the nature of the problem. Chemical and psychological phenomena are threshold phenomena. In principle, either type of phenomenon could trigger the other; and, in particular cases, they could do so to a greater or lesser extent.

The Freudian explanation of psychic disturbance is not necessarily in conflict with an ontological explanation related to man's effort to escape alienation. Indeed, the two may be closely related, for an effort to break down the barriers between individuals or between the individual and nature almost surely has a libidinal as well as an intellectual component. The act of conjugation is the archetypically sexual act; in some species it involves the physical incorporation of the sexual partner and in others the eating of children. Even in humans, biting, an element of the act of eating, is often associated with the sexual act. Even such seemingly perverse sexual activities as beating or scratching involve symbolic incorporation, for they subject the other to the self. The abasement of the partner is the correlate of this act and inversely serves the same function.

Transcending Dysfunction

The real problems facing men are particular problems. These are the problems that provide meaning in men's lives and within the context of which they find their identity as particular human beings. Lives that are productive and creative do not eliminate alienation, but they cope with it and transcend it.

The existence of alien aspects of life is necessary in the problem-solving process. It is the very existence of things beyond our control that enables us to employ control, that is, to change some other things. Thus, the human problem is not the abstract problem of eliminating alienation—for alienation is universally potential in life—but the more particular problem of changing the world in productive and useful ways. Under benign circumstances, particular problems can be solved. Universal aspects of life can never be eliminated and that is why the attempt to overcome them necessarily leads to dysfunction or even to madness.

It is perhaps no accident that the world before creation is thought of as chaos or that in some religions gods are thought of as polymorphous. Alfred North Whitehead may have understood a deep truth when he made his God primordial and unconscious. Consciousness entails thought; thought entails separation; separation entails limitation. Only entities that are limited can be related to other entities. Thus, without the potential for alienation, there cannot be particular lives, human relationships, or solved problems.

Chapter 6

Aspects of Being

The problems of alienation, of authenticity, and of identity are intimately related to the nature of human being. Thus, their elucidation requires at least a minimal inquiry into existential human nature.

The Sensual

One element of being involves a glandular impact on behavior and mind. This operates in two forms: as an impulsion to act upon the world and as a receptivity toward emanations from the world. Anger, fear, love, but also receptivity to sights, sounds, and smells come under this rubric.

Although the particular and the concrete dominate the sensual mode of behavior, they do not exclusively represent it. Smells, sights, and feelings involve perception and not merely sensation. Perception always entails some element of form. However, this element of form can be expressed at the lowest level of abstraction; curve, for instance, rather than space. Even if these low levels of form involve some aspect of mind, it need not be conscious and the levels of form may be biologically embedded. It is a mistake to think of such concepts as the Jungian archetypes as purely unscientific. We know very little about the forms that invest our impulsive behavior, our libidinal motivation, and those aspects of our preconscious thought that are related to them.

This aspect of our being relates us to the most palpable aspects of the external world. This is the anchor that moors us to reality. A supreme designer might have designed the system more sensitively; to detach ourselves from it entirely, however, is equivalent to eliminating our existential basis. We sometimes speak of individuals whose behavior is impulsive as superficial. This is correct from the standpoint of intellect; however, it is intellect that is superficial when divorced from immediate existence. The texture of life—of experience and of action—is intimately related to the richness of the concrete elements of life, even if it is not exclusively determined by them. A personality that does not tap the varieties of concrete, sensuous experience is "thin." In Thomas Mann's *Magic Mountain* both Settembrini and Naphta share these thin qualities. Neither resonates to other people or appears as much more than a walking theory. Their lives have been attenuated.

Rich lives are directly linked to the sensual (as well as to the scientific and to the sacred). The sensual is the realm of the immediate, and gives life its flavor. This realm of life is particular and radically biological. For instance, consider sexual differentiation among animals. The amoeba reproduce by division. Some fish lay their eggs, which are then fertilized externally by the male. Most animals, including humans, reproduce by a specific form of sexual conjugation. The biological differentiation that is fitted to this form of reproduction occurs only after a certain stage in the development of the fetus. Prior to that stage of growth, the fetus is unisexual (female in mammals). This suggests a latent bisexuality, but it also suggests corresponding inhibitory mechanisms that defend this evolutionary jump. If this is the case, then, except in those individuals whose sexual identification is genetically weak, inducement by social and psychological pressures toward perverse forms of sexuality would involve biologically constrained costs. In addition, the biological differentiation between men and women, including nurturing as well as reproductive roles, also is possibly linked to certain types of predispositions as a consequence of evolutionary advantage.

These hypotheses are not necessarily correct and it would frustrate contemporary techniques to attempt to establish them scientifically. Yet it is extremely interesting to note that current discussions of homosexuality and women's liberation are often conducted as if the problem were purely abstract and as if there were no biological linkage.

Even if the foregoing hypotheses are correct, that would be no reason for legal inequality. However, because many people behave in terms of their beliefs concerning the ways in which they ought to behave, an inappropriate understanding of these problems might well induce many individuals to pursue extremely costly lines of behavior. A sufficiently skilled geneticist may someday design an organism in which the female has the protrusive organ, is aggressive about initiating sexual contact, recaptures the fertilized egg, and nurtures it in a detachable external sack. The predispositive sentiments of the males and females of this species may be quite different from those of human males and females. There is nothing in abstract reason that suggests that this should not be the case. Nor is it inconceivable that we could design a biological organism in which both sexes have protrusive but complementary sexual organs, in which contact is initiated bilaterally and in which nurturing occurs externally. The predispositive sentiments of this species likely would be even more different from those of humans as we know them.

From the biological point of view, it is possible that sexual differentiation has led to an innate sense of incompleteness that the individual attempts to overcome. If this speculation has any foundation, it might serve as a partial explanation of some efforts to overcome alienation. Nonetheless, although these efforts may be biologically based, they are biologically impossible. If such an impulse exists, it may even be related to creativity. The impulse to escape separation would lead to activities transforming the self and society. There would be an element of restlessness and rootlessness in the nature of the individual.

We do not suggest that any particular method of making manifest the differentiated sensual tendencies of human nature is necessarily optimal. And we are far from suggesting that particular range of accommodations that the Victorians found. The Victorians were concerned primarily with what differentiated males from females rather than with what they had in common as human beings. If this is correct, Victorian arrangements were likely highly destructive.

There is probably no single univocal set of arrangements that is best, even for an exhaustively specified environment; and environments do differ greatly. Thus, what may have been required in terms of sexual mores for an early industrial culture may be far too constraining for current circumstances. Attempts to prove rigid theses by selective use of evidence from the disorderly history of the species—or from the narrow confines of the primitive social logics we are able to construct with current techniques—are more likely to place external constraints upon the organism than to liberate it. A more eclectic orientation, provided that it is cognizant of the biological being of the human species, is more likely to facilitate adaptive solutions to the problems with which humans need to cope.

Analytical and Theoretical Science

A second aspect of being involves the capacity to employ abstraction and reason analytically and theoretically. This is a large realm extending from simple problem solving to the formal sciences. However, its paradigmatic form is that of theoretical science. Science searches for laws, even if law must be related to boundary conditions.

Science does not deal with the concrete existent. It deals with classes of animals and not with any particular animal. It deals with classes of electrons and not with any particular electron. The existential correlates of the products of this aspect of mind may be palpable in some instances; but abstract generalization is invariably impalpable.

The activities of this aspect of mind may be triggered by an impulse, but the system is operating imperfectly if they are determined by an impulse. Functional separation is required. If these aspects of mind are useful to a society, then the value placed upon them may encourage certain individuals to emphasize them to the exclusion of other aspects of mind. If the generalizations, propositions, or laws formulated by this aspect of mind are treated carelessly, as often happens, the boundary conditions under which they apply may be forgot.

This aspect of mind tends to believe only what can be demonstrated and to respond only to what is not impulsive. If a plane in flight between two cities were suddenly to become self-conscious, it might believe that its function in life was to be continually in flight. If a fuel-regulation system were to become self-conscious, it might believe that the most important objective in life was to control the rate of flow of fuel rather than for the larger system to operate. Yet it is within the self-conscious cortical system of mind that further orders for the operation of the human biological system are formulated; and it may seize control of the entire system.

It has often been asserted that science is the engine of change *par excellence*. The history of the modern world since the origins of theoretical science is cited as support for this proposition. It is surely true that technology is the product of science and that in the modern age technology has produced almost ceaseless social and political change. Yet in a very profound sense the proposition is mistaken. Science introduces a fundamental conservatism.

As Aristotle pointed out, the first technique of science is classification. Classification produces hierarchy and order. Classification excludes. Traditional social systems with closed orders involve early applications of science. Science imposes boundaries and resists change. Science is essentially a scheme for death; for, by increasing the level of abstraction, it continually increases the distance between mind and existence. By insisting upon universals, it attempts to exclude novelty and accident.

What is demonstrated is timeless, for it can never be changed. Yet life is always changing, always overflowing boundaries, always exceeding schemes of classification. It is in this sense that a scheme for controlling nature is a scheme for destroying it, at least if not moderated by other aspects of mind. It is the very fecundity of nature and its resistance to schemes of classification that becomes the challenge.

If we were to construct a control computer to make governmental decisions for us and if this computer became self-conscious, it might begin to control the flow of information to protect its own functioning, thus divorcing itself from a more intimate relationship with the system it was designed to serve. We might have an analogy to the control computer in the activities of some intellectuals whose lives seem to be dominated by the cortical functions of their brains. Entire philosophies have been built around such abstract notions as that colors are not real but that angstrom waves are. The converse error lies in an excessive faith in the sensible, as in the notion that colors are real but that angstrom waves are not. Thus, those whose minds are oriented toward the "concrete" also tend to read all of nature into their particular interpretation of it.

Note carefully the actual character of the metaphor or analogy employed here. Cortical activity is instrumental, but so is perception of the palpable. Glandular and libidinal activity are also instrumental. All structure requires instrumentation. And all successful instrumentation responds to some actual aspect of existence. The error lies in reading the part for the whole. However, the error of the sensible is noted here only to contrast it with the error of the abstract.

I am not arguing for non- or antiscientific premises. Explanation requires science and the use of generalizations. However, I am asserting that there is a tendency on the part of those using scientific method to act as if the entire world consisted only of rarefied abstractions. There is a tendency to forget that an explanation is always an explanation of some thing and that things include emotions, impulses, smells, sights, and other types of concrete phenomena. Science—at least in its confirmatory or explanatory phases—requires strict control. Life, (and creative science as well) cannot stand that much order.

Between science—in its theoretical mode, which invokes the search for testable propositions and theories—and life in the prior sense lies still an additional category that belongs to science at the level of praxis or syncretic thinking. We have earlier explored the area of praxis—the loose equilibrium of the realm of knowledge. The next section explicates praxis from the standpoint of the sacred (for there is an intimate relationship between the two) and attempts to show how this aspect of praxis, as is true in general, is embedded in the character of mind—a conclusion that should not surprise us since all knowledge depends in part upon the character of mind.

The Sacred

The third aspect of being is the sacred. If science requires the formulation of boundary conditions, the sacred requires the stripping away of all conditions. If science depends upon closure, the sacred depends upon holism or all-inclusiveness.

When man attempts to answer the question of who he is or where he belongs in the world, he enters the realm of the sacred. The concrete responds to things as they are existentially. Sciences in the theoretical sense tear things apart in the development of theories. The sacred attempts to restore unity but in a non-immediate sense.

If formal science attempts to differentiate among universals, the sacred attempts to find identities among them. If science stresses functional relationships, the sacred stresses syncretism, consistency, "fittingness," and partial relationships. Yet, as in the case of Mann's Naphta and Settembrini, who both represent death, theoretical science and the sacred have in common timeless being. They represent different modes of expressing truth.

Some religions that represent themselves as standing for revealed truth are non-developmental. Science in its dogmatic form also takes this guise. What are presently understood as the laws of nature are presented as final and ultimate truths. Most scientists are aware that they have no warrant for dogmatic assumptions of this kind. They know that at best they can assert warranted belief in the truth of their current notions of the laws of nature and of their conceptions of science. If the realm of the sacred is regarded as an aspect of being, the understanding of which is pursued by mind, then obviously the same considerations apply to it that apply to the ordinary concerns of science. Indeed, as part of the realm of nature, the sacred, as understood by mind, can be viewed as that aspect of science that is relevant to the search by human beings for the meaning of their existence as this is revealed by the way in which knowledge of man fits with knowledge of society and the physical universe.

Let us examine a few concepts from systems analysis that are relevant to an understanding of the problem. Although they will not give us a precise and complete understanding of the operations of the human mind, they do provide a more precise understanding than ordinary vocabulary permits of the way mind functions in certain respects. They at least point us in the right direction.

Different types of systems are distinguished by the equilibrating processes that occur within them. In the physical sciences, the equilibria primarily are of the mechanical variety. The concept of equality in mechanical equilibria is meaningful because there are independent measures for the variables that have general applicability. Therefore, genuine equalities between them are possible. When we turn to examples of homeostatic equilibria—and all social or political "equilibria" are variations of the homeostatic variety—we no longer have independent measures for genuine equalities. Therefore, the implication of equality in "equilibrium" is not related to covering laws. Hence, the concept of equilibrium is not in this case an explanatory device with respect to "why" questions but is merely a categorizing device that tells us something about "what" we are dealing with.

There are many different types of homeostatic equilibria. The physiological system is homeostatic. For instance, the temperature of the human blood is maintained by processes that compensate for environmental disturbances. In cold weather, constriction of the blood vessels occurs, whereas in hot weather, perspiration takes place. The thermostatic system that maintains room temperature is also homeostatic. When the mercury reaches the desired range, the furnace is turned off. When the mercury goes below the desired range, the furnace is turned on. In both examples, there are related mechanical systems to which the equalities of physics apply within the framework of covering laws. However, homeostatic systems are not systems of equality. The process of perspiration continues until the required temperature change occurs. If, for some reason, this process cannot occur, as would be the case if the human body were covered with paint, either sickness or death would occur. There is no independent measure that will establish the equality between the perspiration and the lowering of temperature.

Some systems are merely homeostatic whereas others are ultrastable or multistable. Consider an ordinary homeostatic system such as the automatic pilot in an airplane. If a plane deviates from level flight while on automatic pilot, the automatic pilot will sense this and, by the application of negative feedback, will adjust the flight pattern of the plane back to level. Consider, however, the case in which the automatic pilot has been incorrectly linked to the ailerons of the plane. If the plane now deviates from level flight, the automatic pilot mechanism will sense this. It will now make an adjustment, but the adjustment, instead of bringing the plane back to level flight, will throw it into a spin. To the extent that purpose implies a capability to pursue a given end by alternative means, this system lacks purpose.

In principle, it would be possible to build an ultrastable automatic pilot the behavior of which was not critically dependent upon the linkages to the ailerons. That is, the automatic pilot could be so built that it would reject its own behavior patterns if these increased the deviations from level flight. It could then "search" for a set of behaviors that would restore the level character of flight. When it found it, it would continue to use it as long as it maintained the critical variable within the established limits for variation. In a sense, this system is capable of adjusting the internal rules by means of which its behavior is governed. This type of ultrastable system would have distinct advantages for survival over a merely stable homeostatic system. Even ultrastability, however, is not sufficient for complex biological survival. W. Ross Ashby, who developed these concepts, therefore applied the term "multistability" to those cases where multiple part functions of the system are individually ultrastable and where they can therefore "search" relatively independently for critical behaviors consistent with the maintenance of the system.

If a visitor from Mars observed the behavior of a machine incorporating the ultrastable automatic pilot suggested by Ashby, its behavior in some respects might seem purposive to him. He would observe it making adjustments in its own internal control system to find an arrangement that would restore level flight to the plane. It would then overcome external obstacles such as large wind gusts in achieving this objective. However, he likely would recognize that this system could not shift from one "purpose" to another, substitute one "purpose" for another, or "choose" a goal that partly matched the perceived requirements. Although further inspection would reveal that the system was designed by an engineer, this would be inessential, for purpose resides in the character of the system rather than in its origin. A being produced by the union of a sperm cell and an ovum, both of which had been designed by a geneticist, would be as "purposeful" as a human produced by "natural" sexual conjugation.

If the visitor from Mars examined the ultrastable system in detail, he would note that it was relatively simple to specify exhaustively the environmental variations to which the machine could adjust. The variable that is to be maintained—namely level flight—would be simple, easily recognizable, and invariant in every environment. It would soon become clear that even if the system were self-conscious, it would never be in any doubt as to its own purpose. Conflict and tragedy would never be part of its internal life. Development or growth of character would be meaningless. It is the continual process of discovery—not of what one is but of what one can become—that gives rise to the concept of the sacred. The concepts of ultrastability and of multistability fall too far short of explicating this. Therefore, we must search for a new concept that expresses the meaning we are searching for.

The term "transfinite stability," or "transstability" for short, will be used for this purpose. It may not be fully adequate, but it at least comes closer than the concepts of ultrastability and multistability. The transfinitely stable system is one with a complex system of purposes. These purposes are not necessarily fully consistent under any environmental circumstance and they give rise to gross conflict under many environmental circumstances. Some, and perhaps most, of these purposes cannot be translated into an easily recognizable and univocal mode of external behavior. The behavior that satisfies the purposes depends upon external conditions. Therefore, information concerning them depends to some extent at least upon knowledge of alternative environments. For individuals, this permits the development of values over time and the building of character. For humanity, it implies a process in history in which learning about human potential takes place. Although every manifestation of this process is finite, no manifestation ever completely satisfies the posited value structure. For every satisfactory state of the world, there is always some potentially superior state. It is in this sense that the process is transfinite.

The incompletion that is an inherent characteristic of any finite state of being gives rise to the quest for completion in a transfinite system. This is primarily the source of the sense of the sacred. This quest becomes perverse when it posits the completion of the search in historical time. In this perverse form, all potential conflicts among goals, all failures of understanding, all alternative tolerable variations of satisfaction, and all human particularities are stripped away. All of life is reduced to particular System. This misconceives and corrupts the character of transfinite process, which is understood only through praxis.

The transfinite process is one of discovery—fundamentally of discovery of what is to be human as this is illuminated by the test in principle. If being human involves being moral—as I believe it does—then transstability is the process by means of which men, in their learning of their humanity, become human and learn how to build a society fit for humans. In this sense, being human involves subjection as well as freedom: subjection to moral rules and consideration for others, and freedom to express one's humanity. Because this transstable process takes place in the realm of praxis, these conceptions develop through comparative understanding of how human behavior, social institutions, culture, and science are linked in alternative possible or real worlds, each of which is characterized by a world view. Thus, a developed conception of humanity is not derived from, or reducible to, any specific theoretical or propositional foundation. It is textured and enriched by the entire web of social existence and deepened by comparative understanding of alternative possibilities. Unlike classical philosophy, however, the standards for this process are objective in Dewey's sense of public communicability and in Peirce's sense of the pragmaticist test. In this sense, the quest for the sacred primarily employs the methods of praxical science (assessment) rather than those of theoretical science.

Differences between Science and the Sacred: Transfinite Stability

We may now further explore the differences between the realm of science and that of the sacred. Although our knowledge of science may develop over time, we normally assume that the laws of science, as distinguished from our knowledge of them, are invariant. Most laws are not developmental. A few cosmological theories appear to be developmental; and our knowledge concerning their invariance is only of low confidence. Human beings live for too short a time to observe the cycle of growth and decay that would occur if one of the competing developmental cosmological theories is correct. However, in principle only one cycle of observation would be required to confirm any specific developmental cosmological theory.

Knowledge of human nature is not in principle penetrable through the intensive study of a single cycle of development. Human nature develops (either progressively or retrogressively) as we learn about ourselves under different external and informational conditions. This dependence upon comparative information does not make the subject of human nature totally recalcitrant to study. However, this dependence upon a comparative historical record implies a development of that which is under study such that knowledge cannot in principle be complete within historical time, let alone within a single human cycle. This does not mean that all reasonable inferences are impossible but only that the level of confidence we achieve will be low. Man is not a book to be read at one sitting, and the reading that finally occurs will be to some extent at least dependent upon historical accidents.

From this perspective, we perpetually make discoveries about human nature and society. As we learn about ourselves, sometimes erroneously, the sense arises within us of a moral imperative. In this way our nature speaks to us of the things that we must do. Recognition of this need, of this aspect of being, is an inherent element in its utilization. If and when such recognition occurs, men who are constrained from acting according to moral necessity will recognize themselves as unfree.

Transfinitely stable systems always involve compromises, for there must always be sacrifice with respect to some value in order to achieve some gain with respect to another value. For instance, love is sacrificed for honor or vice versa. This is necessarily true in an environment with sufficient variety to provide genuine choice. If the environment is sufficiently benign, then the price paid with respect to any particular value may be small. In this case, strong characters would be capable of fully facing the facts. However, during history, few environments have been benign. To achieve some goals, severe prices have had to be paid with respect to others.

Even people not ostensibly reduced to such conflicts of choice in severe environments have been forced to restrict their human sympathy for those in less fortunate circumstances. If, as some have hypothesized, human sympathy and the recognition of the sacred in each of us are basic elements of our character, then the psychological mechanism of denial is required. Whatever one may think of this particular example, if he can construct some other example to the same point, it will become evident that techniques for the exclusion of information are required by such systems if they are to maintain internal psychic equilibrium. Their attention then becomes diverted to other gains—the kinds of gains Freud termed secondary—which are then perceived as if they were primary. In addition, human beings go through a long period of learning. If they learn inefficiently, they may fear striking out on more productive paths. In this case also, they learn to value secondary gains.

I do not wish to push this discussion too far, as the investigation of the mechanisms of information regulation are not directly pertinent to this inquiry. However, it is important to recognize that transstable systems do employ information-processing mechanisms and that they can become dysfunctional. Thus, many problems can arise from the misprocessing of information. Among these problems some of the most severe are those we have already discussed: those dealing with the elimination of alienation. Because of faulty inferences, because examples are often employed without consideration of differences in boundary or environmental conditions, because inherent limitations are sometimes imaginatively stripped away, inherently infeasible and destructive quests are initiated. It requires only the adding of a suffix such as "less" to a word such as "time" to believe that one imagines a timeless entity having an existence similar to that of concrete being or the adding of the word "overcoming" to "separation" to convince oneself that all limitations of existential being can be overcome.

Transstable systems never overcome limitation. However, they are capable of a development that better fulfills the necessity of their own being. They are capable in most environments of finding ways to a productive existence and of making changes in the environment such that their prospects are improved.

Transstability and Search Procedures

The transstable system requires much more sophisticated search procedures than the ultrastable system. In the first place, it must seek to interact with a much more variable relevant environment. In the second place, the set of requirements it must satisfy is far more complex. In the third place, it does not possess a set series of responses that can be tried in serial or random fashion. The internal system and the external environment are simultaneously complexly variable. The combinatorial potential is astronomical. Any systematic search procedure at the conscious level, even a relatively random one, would likely overwhelm the organism and incapacitate it for its daily tasks.

Even if we speak metaphorically and speculatively, there is probably a very complicated division of labor in transstable systems in which most of the search procedures occur at a preconscious level. The kind of signaling or recognition device that is required for determining the admission to the level of consciousness of possible solutions that are worthy of consideration is not even hinted at in the current literature on brain functioning. We do not even begin to suspect how this combinatorial search is triggered off either by conscious activity or by some other form of bodily impulse. We do not know how the conscious mind decides which of the hypothetical solutions that rise from the preconscious level are worth systematic scientific investigation. Some process of recognition and identification, and perhaps of reasoning, is involved, but we do not know that the primitive methods we are now employing in the coding of computers bears any significant relationship to it.

Chapter 7

Identification

Identification and Alienation

Perhaps the reader wishes a concrete discussion of identification. I cannot oblige him in a work of this kind. What we identify with depends on the realm of knowledge and our location in it. As the former differs with time and place and the latter with the individual, the problem of identification can only be discussed in detail if the scope of reference is strictly bounded. Yet such a bounded discussion would be irrelevant to this book.

Although the ethologists may overgeneralize this point, imprinting may lead a duckling to identify with the human who takes it as the egg hatches. The process by which bonds of relationship become internalized by humans and the reasons that are acceptable in justifying these relationships will differ with time and place. The consistancy and "fit" of the realm of praxis provide the constraints within which the process operates. Anything beyond a general discussion of the concept would take us beyond the confines of this book.

159

Identification involves a sense of membership: in a species, a nation, or a family, for instance. Membership implies differentiation from other membership groupings. Identity involves an individual history and, in particular, a history in which problems are overcome by a particular being. Particular histories are always differentiated from other particular histories. And alienation is always induced by a disjunction between an identification and the relationship it makes relevant to the self.

To understand the importance of a sense of identity in coping with alienation, it may be useful to contrast Adam Smith's use of "alienation" with Karl Marx's. When Adam Smith asserted that the worker in industry was pursuing a meaningless task, he meant that the worker was unable to perceive a meaningful relationship between his portion of the task and the finished product, whereas the artisan carried the task of production through from beginning to end. When Marx spoke of commodity fetishism and the alienation of the worker, he was indulging in a romantic confusion. The subjective concern of the worker with the problem of his alienation, to the extent that it exists at all, does not arise from the fact that he is paid a salary directly related to his economic input into the productive process. Most workers are concerned primarily with their well-being and not with the problem Marx discusses. To the extent that some workers are alienated, this stems primarily from the fact that under many forms of market economy they are subject to cycles of business over which they lack individual control. It may also arise from the fact that workers have no competence to deal with major accidents: great depressions, terrible illnesses, floods or hurricanes, or other social or natural catastrophes. Under these circumstances, some workers may perceive themselves as prisoners of fate who are treated as objects of life and who therefore lack dignity.

The problem discussed by Adam Smith can be overcome only if we are willing to dispense with the mass manufacture of products. The problem discussed by Marx cannot be solved in his terms. However, if we take a more specific view of alienation, there are alternative methods for attempting to cope with it. State ownership of industry is one method. Welfare legislation is another. The Yugoslav experiment in worker management and the reputed Japanese practice of consensus-building in management (to the extent that it really exists) are others. In none of these cases can we eliminate alienation as a general phenomenon or even alienation in work. However, we may be able to increase the control that man has over his destiny and to improve his subjective sense of dignity and, therefore, of himself as an identifiable, autonomous individual.

As man is linked to other men in institutional structures— and to the rules, moral or otherwise, that characterize them— his life acquires meaning and specific goals are legitimized (in the absence of which the definition of rationality as optimization of preferences has no real-world referent).

As these existential identity factors change, the criteria by means of which goals (and individuals) are evaluated change also. We change both the problems that people face and the potential solutions that attend them. But we can never eliminate problems and the potential alienation that new identifications will make relevant to the human condition.

The attempt to overcome alienation in general represents an attempt to achieve perfection in life. However, existence is always necessarily flawed. When we ignore this, we indulge in a flight of fancy that removes words from their mooring in particularity. Utopias of this type are not peopled with real individuals with real conflicting interests. They are peopled by phantoms of the imagination: and necessarily of the conscious imagination, for the phantoms of dreams often act contrary to the wishes of the dreamer. Marx, alas, suffered (at least in one common interpretation of his position) from the disordered dream that conflict could be removed from life and that then true history would begin, whereas the real problem in life is that of arranging conflicts in the most productive and least harmful fashion. We rearrange them, not to eliminate alienation, but to reestablish identity. In that way, we reduce anxiety and, perhaps, if we are lucky, eliminate anguish and despair.

Identity and Anxiety

Emphasis on a sense of identity has been stressed so often that it has become banal. Psychologists note that those with a poor sense of identity suffer from anxiety in situations that "normal" people accept calmly. This should surprise no one. Systems with a self-conscious internal governor require the interposition of cognitive decision processes between motivation and behavior. In short, they must find some rule for action. A rule is not helpful if there is no way to choose between it and a conflicting rule. Thus, a human actor needs knowledge of the environment and of the objective that a rule is designed to serve. The formal rule, for instance, that citizens should serve their country could not be applied unless the person employing the rule knew of which country he is a citizen. If this is obscure to him, or if he must choose from among conflicting rules, he does not know how to behave. His anxiety is a manifestation of this indecision. He is impelled alternatively to various courses of action, none of which seems satisfactory and each of which, at least for a period of time, rises to the level of consideration only ultimately to be rejected. Perhaps toward the end of this process he is driven toward an impulsive action which is again a source of anxiety as he reflects upon it. Anxiety is an ontological necessity in a system that is self-reflexive; that employs goal-oriented actions; and that lacks awareness of rules, the criteria for choice from among conflicting rules, or a means of employing them that is relevant to its existential situation. Anomie thus tends to accompany a lack of identity; and the overcoming of anxiety requires the finding of meaning and of identity.

Meaning and Identity

Meaning always includes definite reference, even if the reference is to an abstraction. There is no such thing as meaning in general or meaning that is abstracted from all relationships. There are no rules that are valuable or valid in general. There are only rules that are valuable or valid in particular types of circumstances. Light has meaning only in relation to darkness. Words have meaning only in relation to the meanings of other words and to the syntactical structure of language. The meaning of an action requires knowledge of the context in which it occurs. Laughter at a comedy does not have the same meaning as laughter at the agony of another individual. Parallel lines do not mean the same thing in Euclidean and non-Euclidean geometry. A gesture does not mean the same thing when a friend makes it that it means when an enemy makes it. An offer to arbitrate a dispute does not mean the same thing after years of litigation that it means at the beginning of a dispute.

For life to have meaning and for an individual to have identity, there must be ordered sets of relationships within which particular actions have meaning. These ordered structures include the physical, the biological, the psychological, the social, the economic, and the political. Even within the narrower realm of the social, the political, and the economic, the most violent revolutionaries never dared change many of these elements at once.

This should not surprise us. The tool we use to build a piece of furniture would not be useful if its shape and form changed under our hands. We could not think if the significance of words changed as we used them. This does not mean that we cannot form different tools with different shapes or even pound our present tools into alternative shapes. It does not mean that we cannot change the significance of some words at one time and of many words over longer times. It does mean that the changes can be meaningful only if the general framework within which they occur is relatively unchanged, in the short term at least.

Our sense of identity and the meaning we achieve in life depend upon the persistence of form and structure. Yet it is form and structure that permit alienation, for it cannot exist in the formless. The purposeful individual lives a life filled with meaning because his subjective awareness is directed more to the identifications in his life than to the alienations.

Identity therefore depends upon the continuities in life, including primarily those that affect one's defined roles. (Of course, the understanding of identities is enriched by comparison with differences.) A person has expectations about the behavior of others and about the states of the world. As long as these beliefs about the world accord with experience, or are rationalized subjectively, the individual will maintain a sense of identity. If doubts arise about these expectations, anxiety will develop with respect to those roles and institutions to which the doubts apply; and there will be a tendency to anomie in these areas.

Because of the importance to an individual of his sense of identity, his belief in it is often protected by dysfunctional regulatory mechanisms that resist with greater or lesser effectiveness information to the contrary streaming either from the environment or from internal aspects of the personality system. Thus, a sense of identity may be consistent with inauthenticity and great impoverishment of character. In malign environments, a sense of identity may even depend upon inauthenticity of character or personality except in the most philosophically wise individuals.

Identity and Traditional Society

The sense of identity seems open to least doubt within traditional societies. Traditional societies tend to be hierarchical; and, if they have plural hierarchies, these tend to be consistent with each other. Changes of individual status within a hierarchical structure tend to follow prescribed paths. The rules of behavior change extremely slowly. They are usually highly specific—and thus easily applicable—rather than general. Traditional societies also employ ritual; and rituals symbolically relate man to a group and to the universe. Symbolism has meaning at the intellectual level, but it also has meaning at the sensual level. Rhythms, melodies, colors, artistic forms, dances, intonations, and gestures play roles in reinforcing the bonds among men and nature. Traditional societies often provide great dignity to the individual, at least with respect to those in the ranks to which honor accrues. Dignity includes a sense of worth and thus confers a sense of identity. However, the sense of identity in these societies will not be transstable, for the framework of comparison is extremely limited.

The Sense of Identity and Modernity

The workers of whom Adam Smith wrote or those whom Marx called alienated more accurately lacked a stable sense of identity, for the former could not identify with the task they performed and the latter could not identify with a world that treated them as flotsam on the waves of economic distress. The former performed by rote a mechanical operation that they could not relate to the larger system in which it occurred. The latter found their value as human beings changing rapidly with the vagaries of economic dislocations of which they had little understanding and over which they had little control. Within these aspects of their human experience, they had lost their sense of orienation. The former had no sense of the worth of what they were doing and the latter had no consistent sense of their worth. Their sense of identity was fractured.

To categorize such phenomena as instances of alienation is to grossly misunderstand them and to seek a solution to the wrong problem. The problem is not one of eliminating alienation; it is rather one of recreating a sense of identity. The former conceptualization of the process sends one in search of an apocalyptic solution—a solution that is ontologically impossible. The latter conceptualization of the process requires an examination of the specific processes of socialization and of production within a society in the search for those specific transformations most consistent with a sense of individual identity.

Identity and Transfinite Stability

So far I have dealt with the conception of identity at the simplest level. Expressed so simply, it would seem to suggest a restoration of a previous golden age, of a search for traditional forms. Although such a conclusion is not incorrect merely because it is impossible under current conditions—for tribalism can never mean in industrial society what it meant under pastoral conditions—that way of conceptualizing the process is excessively narrow. If one examines the concept of identity from the standpoint of human potentiality, the sense of identity under traditional conditions is seen to be extremely restricted. Identity, more fully understood, involves the relationship of an individual to the social systems or subsystems that are relevant to his membership roles, his place in a hierarchy of being, and his responsibilities and prerequisites as a social actor. The last involves the relationship of an action to a rule or of a rule to the set or sets of rules relevant to behavior, the conditions under which rules are applied, the conditions under which rules change, and the conditions under which changes in the sets of rules occur. With the last qualification, transstability is required. (The way in which taste adds to transfinitely stable identity will be discussed in the last chapter.)

Transstable behavior requires a sophisticated intellect. The sense of identity in modern society breaks down if an individual either cannot or does not know how to make appropriate transstable distinctions. For example, it is often asked why the use of force within a nation is not justifiable if its use by a nation against other nations is justified. Without attempting to answer that question in any absolute way—or even to argue that under no circumstances should force be used within the nation—it is surely legitimate to respond that the characteristics of a centralized polity differ so much from those of a decentralized one that it is similar expectations with respect to the use of force that require justification. It is sometimes argued, for instance, that because war is cruel no one should be punished for extreme cruelty during war or that everyone should be punished for engaging in cruel actions. This argument fails to distinguish appropriate differences in the applicability of rules under different sets of conditions. If accepted, it would interfere with an effort to maintain any standards with respect to the use of force in war either directly, as in the first formulation of the argument, or indirectly, with respect to the second formulation, as a consequence of the impracticability of the standard.

Modern society creates problems that impair the sense of identity of many individuals who lack an effective transstable personality. Events may move so swiftly that they lack the intellectual or emotional capacity to relate to them in any meaningful way. Events beyond their control may fragment their lives and make meaningless to them their relationships to institutions of which they are defined members. If their tasks are taken over by animals or machines, even their sense of identity as human beings may become attenuated.

Modern society thus includes many types of individuals with many different types of identity problems. Individuals who follow rules only to gain the approval of other people lack a sense of identity. Individuals who pursue objectives exclusively for self-gain have a diminished sense of identity, for they have a diminished capability for identifying either with particular institutions or with society as a whole. Individuals who compulsively follow rules regardless of external circumstances have a diminished sense of identity, for that kind of rule-controlled behavior becomes a crutch without which the individual is unable to function.

Thus modernity creates serious problems for individuals who lack transstable personalities—problems that diminish their identification with important elements of society and that tend to produce anomie with respect to these. If authentic behavior responds to all aspects of being—and that is the theme of the next chapter—a society that produces transstable personalities will also produce authentic men. However, transstable identity and authenticity are independent, if related, concepts. Conceivably a price must always be paid in terms of one for a gain in terms of the other. This price would likely be greater in some conditions than in others. Whereas, for instance, puritanical individuals may have a distinct sense of identity in puritanical culture, the penalties of law and custom that would be applied to authentic humans in such a culture might shatter their sense of identity unless they had the strongest of personalities and the most philosophic of minds. Similar shocks might await a moral person in an exclusively pleasure-seeking society. However, appropriate social and natural conditions may decrease the conflict between identity and authenticity and permit major improvements in the manifestations of both. Both are requirements of being.

Identity and Justice

As stated in *Justice, Human Nature, and Political Obligation,* the process of identification is an important key to the applicability of moral rules. The identifications of a man—and his resolution of conflicts between them—depend upon understanding, socialization, and environmental conditions. It would have been silly to have asked a sixteenth-century Frenchman to behave as a world citizen, because, except in a very peripheral sense, that concept would have been irrelevant to the moral choices facing him. Moreover, there is not necessarily a univocal hierarchy among identifications; for a man appropriately may decide to identify as a world citizen with respect to ecological matters and as a national citizen with respect to more narrowly conceived national security interests.

To the extent that important moral choices involve conflicts among actual or potential identifications, they are at least partly relative in the sense developed in chapter 3 of *Justice, Human Nature, and Political Obligation*. To the extent that these conflicts involve identifications the individual has internalized strongly, such moral conflicts will alienate him. The solutions he finds for this alienation—repression, sublimation, affective isolation, reconstruction of institutions—depend upon understanding and the means at hand; and some will worsen rather than improve the condition. These latter aspects—understanding and the means at hand—will determine the arrangement of values and normative rules best suited to these circumstances.

How identifications relate to alienation and justice, therefore, is kaleidoscopic. The realm is one of praxis. No theory can be developed that can be applied provided only that enough is known about initial conditions. And philosophical theories that pretend to answer problems concerned with values or alienation in this fashion are illusory.

Chapter 8

Authenticity

The Particular and the General

Sometimes destructive actions that issue from hostile emotions are called genuine or authentic and they are contrasted with hypocritical good manners that respond to social custom from habit or fear. However authentically such destruction may represent a particular emotional feeling, it is not clear that it authentically represents man, for such a view reduces man to his momentary passions. Yet, these may stand between him and authentic action as surely as social hypocrisy on occasion does. Being is both particular and general. With evolutionary development, complexity of structure increasingly permitted an elaboration in the complexity of the interactive processes of society. With the elaboration of the cortical aspects of neurological structures, complexity became possible not merely in the particularities of interactions but in the intellectual understanding of them as well. Behavior is not authentic unless it genuinely represents this.

Cortical Complexity and Inauthentic Behavior

Cortical development in man introduced an extremely powerful control factor, or governor, for the system: a governor that became capable of suppressing important aspects of human nature and of diminishing its richness. The power of anticipation introduces the possibility of foresightful fear. Because of the particularities of individual nurture or social experience, various aspects of human motivation, thought, and social behavior can be repressed or "outlawed." The life of feeling, of mind, and of interactive behavior can be impoverished. Men become blind to the play of light and color, deaf to the harmonies and cacophonies of sound, insensitive to the varieties of taste, immune to the feelings of love and hate, resistant to the joys of thought, incapable of arguing in a logical manner, insensitive to the distinction between their interests and those of others, incapable of recognizing the autonomy of others, and blind to the shortness of human life and the infinity of its worth.

In some men, impoverishment may extend over almost the entire range of being. In others, impoverishment in some aspects may coexist with exaggerated development in others. The decadents of the *Yellow Book* period and the "crazies" who do their own thing regardless of the consequences for others are examples of the latter phenomenon: that of an impoverishment of one aspect of being and an exaggerated development of another. Those who are impoverished lack authenticity. Their behavior does not stem directly from the nature of their being, but is distorted or rerouted by an intellectual belief, or an emotional blockage, or a defense mechanism.

Some might argue that both defense mechanisms and mental concepts are part of being and therefore that even impoverished individuals respond authentically. Note, however, the crucial difference between the decision or the defense mechanism that permits the expression of being through mediation, or that delays a mode of action until it can be safely employed, on the one hand, and that which forecloses its use, on the other. If one fears a specific danger and runs to a safe place where he can engage in other activities, that is quite distinct from possession of a fear that becomes so generalized that behavior becomes one long flight. There is a difference between the type of thinking that solves a problem, whether that problem is concrete or intellectual, and thought processes that are as diversionary as the fear that leads to constant running. In each case the motivation has been torn from its particular nexus, has been generalized, and acquires a life of its own that is independent and that "locks up" the behavior of the individual.

Think of an electric organ with a toy organ on top of it. Divert the wiring of the apparatus so that when the keys of the electric organ are played, it is the toy organ that sounds. What one hears now may be the authentic sound of the toy organ; but it is not the authentic voice of the electric organ. It is not the fact of alteration that makes for inauthenticity but the type of alteration. The fact that these distinctions are easier to make with respect to simpler systems—and that in the case of the organ the system is designed—should not obscure the fact that the distinction is real. And, by the test in principle, it would not be chosen by the person.

Impoverished behavior, therefore, is inauthentic. In the case of the literary decadents of the *Yellow Book* period, who explored the senses in such great detail, their behavior responds to an aspect of being. However, the decadent individual was inauthentic, for he closed off an essential aspect of his humanity. Think of a thermostatic heating system that operates in the following manner: when the temperature is too low, the thermostat turns the heating equipment on and the temperature continues to increase until the thermostat turns off. The thermostat now turns on the equipment and the temperature starts going up. However, the linkage between the thermostat and the heater is now cut off. The heater consequently continues to increase the temperature, at least until an explosion or some other accident occurs. The heater could be said to be behaving authentically but the thermostatic heating system is no longer behaving authentically. The test in principle of *Justice, Human Nature, and Political Obligation* provides the key for making the appropriate distinctions.

Control systems, rather than being inconsistent with authenticity, are essential elements of authenticity in the case of transstable systems. It is the type of linkage among the elements of the system that determines whether it is behaving authentically or not.

Although control systems, including the application of moral rules, are essential elements in authentic human behavior, not every application of control is consistent with authenticity. Chapter 5 examined various dysfunctions of mind, including the obsessive-compulsive. Many of these aberrations involve control mechanisms that have not been integrated into the human personality. For instance, some people may follow moral rules only because they have calculated that they will gain from doing so. Although they may obey moral rules, and although this may be better for society than if they did not, the moral rules are not an integral part of their personality but are superimposed upon it. In this sense, their behavior lacks authenticity.

Although the human system is so complicated that confident generalizations about its nature are reckless, our ability to distinguish authentic from inauthentic human beings is, if far less than perfect, still far better than random. At least with respect to the emotional areas of life, it is not too difficult to distinguish, for instance, between individuals in contact with their libidinal mainsprings and those who are not. The authentic individual taps all areas of his being; and they are integrated into his personality.

Authenticity and "Balance"

I recognize, as I have stated previously many times, that the aspects of being are not entirely harmonious and that under unfortunate environmental conditions tragic conflicts of choice may be presented. The authentic man is not one who maximizes each aspect of his being, for that is patently impossible. However, he is a man who is not cut off from contact—as metaphorical as these words may be—with all the aspects of his being: the sensual, the intellectual, the sacred, the moral, and the creative. Yet, authentic man does not simply resonate, for there is a necessary interposition—the intellectual and the moral—between the expression of his desire and his judgment of its value.

This conception of authenticity obviously has much in common with Aristotle's concept of "balance," or even with Plato's discussion of the three aspects of being, or with psychoanalytical conceptions of the adjusted man. This should not be entirely surprising. It is rather late in the intellectual history of man to come up with an entirely new conception of the nature of mankind. However, there are a number of differences as well.

The nature of man is not something that can become known within isolated social settings. Comparative knowledge is necessary, for only comparative knowledge can relate behavior to the environmental constraints under which it occurs. Only comparative analysis can factor out the relationships between choices made and the constraints determining the character of the alternatives. Only a wide enough range of comparisons with other choices within the same social system and with other choices within different social systems can permit one systematically to investigate the moral consequences of different kinds of choices. Moreover, the framework of analysis employed in this book and in *Justice, Human Nature, and Political Obligation* clarifies the fact that justice is a developmental concept. This emphasizes the need for a continual reassessment of the justification of social, political, and economic arrangements.

Authenticity and Alienation

Rather than being antithetical to alienation as some writers believe, authenticity requires alienation, at least potentially and perhaps actually. It does so in an ontological sense, in a biological sense, and in a moral sense. The concept of "self" would be meaningless without the concept of "other." Unity requires distinction and distinction requires unity. Hunger requires food external to the body. Love requires an external lover. Intellect requires a subject matter. Games require opponents. And morality requires a moral other for its meaning.

Would a love subject to our control be worth winning? If the laws of nature were subject to our whim, would they be worth studying? If our opponent threw the match, would the game be worth winning? If our arbitrary will determined the rights of others, would our moral stature be worth possessing?

The work of art when complete is beyond the will of the artist. If our children are to be moral works of art, they must become autonomous and freed from our moral control, although not necessarily from meaningful relationships with us. If our students are to be educated, they must become scholars in their own right and forever freed from our opinions.

We can express our nature, that is, behave authentically, only as we free our works from ourselves. And this process makes alienation likely in a complex environment. When we fail to free our works, our children, and our students from ourselves, we initiate dysfunctional mechanisms of regulation that impoverish us and those we seek to help in community with us.

And yet such dysfunctional attempts must fail, for they increase our alienation from our own being and destroy the community of interest we might have had with genuinely independent others. Alienation cannot be eliminated. The attempt to eliminate it impoverishes the expression of being. Thus, perhaps it would be more precise to say that authenticity requires the acceptance of alienation both as a potentiality and as at least an occasional occurrence.

Chapter 9

Creativity, Productivity, Style, and Justice

Creativity

Creativity can become manifest in almost every type of activity: the design of a new style of architecture, the proof of a new mathematical proposition, the invention of a new gadget, the discovery of a new concept, the invention of a new game, a new deployment in chess or war, or the coining of a new word or expression.

Creative Thought and the Preconscious

Creative thought occurs at the preconscious level. The techniques of mathematical, logical, and linguistic analysis that we apply to the confirmation of theories or of praxical consistency are necessarily conscious and orderly. These aspects permit the public communicability that is essential to science. However, those aspects of judgments that underlie the assessment and reassessment of any field of knowledge—

179

whether of science, morals, literature, or art—are not fully amenable to this conscious process. They require a widespread search activity and a recognition of "fittingness" that is sometimes based on a reordering of the entire field. This reordering may occur because the preconscious recognizes possibilities for greater relatedness—or for eliminating inconsistencies—in the field that others have failed to detect or because new information reveals these possibilities. In the latter case, the creative person is the one who is preconsciously alert to these potentials. This reordering is then subject to the procedures of public (objective) communication. For instance, we may test specific propositions for theories and organize evidence assigned to argue for the "fit" of the new theory or proposition in a reordered field. But this is an *a posteriori* process.

In creative individuals the (metaphorical) barrier between the preconscious and the conscious is very permeable. A barrier between the preconscious and the conscious obviously is required, or the flow of ideas would interfere with the reasoning of conscious thought: a reasoning that is directed toward constructive action on the basis of communicable experience or confirmed hypothesis. There also would be social costs if no barrier existed. Too many suggestions for change would undermine the perceived certainties that provide social sanction for accepted norms, in the absence of which predictable behavior would not be possible. Some degree of creativity has evolutionary advantage, but only up to a point.

However, mechanisms of social control may punish the use of creative thought and may "raise" the "barrier" higher than evolutionary necessity demands. Moreover, there may be conflicts between the macro- and microneeds of society. For instance, parents may repress a curiosity seemingly disadvantageous to the family so thoroughly that insufficient creative talent is available to society. This may diminish an aspect of being and produce an unnecessary degree of alienation.

Although science and conscious thought seek precision in the meaning of words, the creative process thrives on ambiguity in meaning. The confusions produced by ambiguity are amply compensated for by the richness of the creative associations and identifications that are triggered by them. However, there must be some restriction on ambiguity: otherwise there would not be sufficient differentiation among concepts for associations to be meaningful. The preconscious requires some degree of differentiation for creativity. Consequently, the preconscious also is a potential source of alienation. Because, however, it focuses more on identities than on differences, the preconscious is not likely the major source of alienation that many writers believe it to be.

Creativity and Alienation

Those who are alienated from society in general or from a particular elite group may be more receptive to a lowering of the threshold between preconscious and conscious thought than those who are comfortably "adapted." They may be disposed to search for a new unity as a form of rejection of, or opposition to, the old perceived disunity. That the sense of alienation is not a sufficient condition for creative activity, however, is amply shown by the fact that many people who feel alienated are not creative.

Some people may develop creative traits from a negative predisposition. They may then discover a strong affirmative fulfillment in artistically or socially productive activities that becomes an autonomous motive for their continuation. Alienation, therefore, may not be a necessary condition for creativity any more than it is a sufficient condition.

Transfinitely stable people with a strong sense of identity also may be disposed to search for new modes of expression or of social organization. They may be creative from a strongly affirmative quest for novelty in expression, improvement in their conditions of life, or improvement of the human condition in general. Recognizing that life is inevitably imperfect, they may accept the present as a reasonable set of "solutions" and still be strongly disposed to seek productive solutions to the problems, either personal or social, that remain unsolved. They may respond to transformations of society under new conditions, and to the new problems that arise from present "solutions."

Creative Style and Its Cycle

In the arts and literature, creativity seems to go through cycles of style. Thus, a romantic movement may give rise to an intellectual one: representational art may be followed by abstract art, or impressionism by metaphysical painting, and metaphysical painting by actionism.

Although art is superficially a sensuous activity, the history of art makes manifest the great differences in the temperaments of artists: in some periods art reflects the warmness of passion; in others it manifests the coldness of intellect; and, in still others the pure spirit of religious or moral ideals becomes evident. In some periods sensibility and fineness of detail are emphasized; in others simplicity and comprehensibility take a leading role.

These trends appear to occur in cycles, and we do not begin to understand the reasons for them. However, there are a number of convenient hypotheses that initially seem promising. The newer a mode of activity, the more extensive it would seem are the innovations that can be pursued within it. Thus, for instance, in the realm of science the major inventions of Galileo, Newton, Planck, and Einstein opened up vast new areas of scientific activity. In the same way, artistic innovations open up possibilities for other artists. Regardless of how the preconscious creative process may operate, the more open the terrain it explores—provided it is not chaotic— the more likely that creative discovery will occur.

Whether a major innovation finds a social response may

depend upon a number of factors. There must be a readiness for it somewhere within the system. The discoveries of Galileo permitted successful experimentation by others. The vast conceptions of Newton permitted a meaningful explanation of diverse phenomena that were of interest to scientists and philosophers. The public may have hooted at Beethoven's music, but the musical avant-garde was ready for it. Moreover, his musical romanticism coincided with strong romantic movements in literature and in popular feeling.

As these new movements continued, their very success diminished the scope for further creativity within the same framework. On the other hand, their success encouraged others to continue to mine these fields until they ran out, as in many of the western gold rushes in the United States. As these motivating factors moved toward their margins, the interplay of motivations likely again favored those searching for new breakthroughs, although only particular efforts would combine novelty with public readiness in a manner productive of success.

From the standpoint of the consumers of art, much of the same motivational pattern may apply. The newer the movement, the richer the rewards to be gained by those who consume its products. As the rewards begin to diminish, novelty declines and acceptance increases. Finally, an important section of the public is sated and waits for something new.

Cultural innovations may initiate a similar pattern in the style of social life. With the introduction of a new style, one has a feeling of breaking through the constraints of past styles and of being liberated by the new. As time goes on, the style is sanctified by public acceptance. Ultimately the once new is perceived as a set of rigidified forms within which changes can occur only in small ways and at the margin. It is now experienced as a constraint on conduct and its costs rather than its rewards are at the focus of attention.

Creative Style and Authenticity

This tentative explanation would be merely interesting except for one possible problem. If expression of the three major aspects of being—the sensual, the intellectual, and the sacred—is essential if humans are to achieve authenticity, the cyclic process we are describing may result in cyclic inauthenticity and impoverishment of character. Yet, if the hypotheses concerning them are correct, there may be a semi-independent process generating them that it would be most difficult to control, especially under modern conditions.

Is this problem ineluctable? Although that question is fundamental, I doubt that it can be answered on the basis of existing evidence. However, even before attempting a hypothetical and very speculative answer to that problem, the related problem of productivity will be discussed.

Productivity

We use metaphors such as "breakthrough" and recombinations of particulars to stress what we mean by creation. Productivity might then simply be regarded as repetitive activity. In this sense, we would call an artist's painting creative and the work of a punch press operator merely productive.

We have a clear distinction in these two examples, but it is not clear that we have chosen the right examples. The punch press is a non-ultrastable machine. Consider the simplest type of ultrastable machine: Ashby's postulated automatic pilot. Is it creative when it readjusts its own internal connections to achieve level flight? What happens when we move to transstable cases: for instance, human beings? Is the salesman merely productive or is he creative as he sells his packages of hairpins from door to door? Is a traditional art that follows stylized form creative or merely productive? Is the maker of kitsch for Woolworth merely a producer? Is the policeman arresting a drunk merely a producer? Is the writer of a hack textbook who plagiarizes other sources merely a producer?

Our problem stems from the fact that although we can establish a distinction between creativity and productivity without too much trouble, no human activity is purely one or the other. Yet, if we wish to characterize human behavior, we need both terms, often for the same acts. There are great creative artists who are not productive: that is, they are original but they do not produce a large body of work. And there are very productive artists who are not very creative.

There is still another, and more important, sense in which activity may be said to be productive. Merely repetitive activity may produce a useless output. Some activity, however, copes more or less adequately with real problems. Thus, increasing sales by a salesman may "solve" his family's economic problems. Increasing production by industry may "solve" a consumption problem. Acquiring friends may "solve" a personality problem. Receptivity to a stylistic change in society is evidence that the new style responds productively to some real need even though we may be unable to articulate that need and even though the "solution" may create worse problems than it "solves."

Changes in Productive Style

There are stylistic differences in productive activities as well as in creative ones. However, these do not seem to be cyclical in the sense that we noted in the case of creativity (at least for the elite). We do not deny the recurrence of some features of social style. Through much of human history we can note an alternation between the heroic and the religious spirits. Overlapping that dyad, almost as in a counterpoint, was the cycle of mercy and justice, sometimes as represented in moon (goddess, Marian) cults and sun (god, Jesus) cults.

Werner Sombart thought he detected an alternation of warrior and bourgeois spirits in the modern world. Max Weber was concerned with the rise of the bourgeois mentality and much of modern social science follows him in this. Much of the social ferment in the first half of the twentieth century involved a romantic rejection of the bourgeois spirit; indeed, much of the new left movement of today reacts to bourgeois values as did the protofascist movements of the 1920s and 1930s.

However, as long as we avoid the unilinear fallacy, social style seems to be developmental. The managerial and the scientific productive mentalities arose within the bosom of the bourgeois mentality. As capitalism developed, the reward structure of society fostered those mentalities that could make it work. As capitalism became dependent upon management and science, the incentive structure changed, thus partly eliciting a change in the productive mentalities of the period.

Although Adam Smith saw the relatively unskilled factory worker's job as meaningless—a theme repeated much later with graphic effectiveness in Charlie Chaplin's *Modern Times*—this did not correctly express the perception of the average worker. He did not think of his work primarily from the standpoint of its relationship to the completed product. His perception of himself during an era of scarcity was of a man contributing to the prosperity of the country and to the welfare of his family. Thus, contrary to what Adam Smith thought, the worker could have a sense of identity and could take some pride in his work, although perhaps not as much as that of the artisan whose work was often satisfying in its own terms.

With the rise of an affluent society, a welfare system, an availability of jobs for married women, a multiplicity of jobs for men, and an expansion of service activities that are not productive in the material sense, the relatively unskilled factory worker found it much more difficult to perceive a meaningful relationship between his work and a worthy role in the social system. His family's dependence on his labor was reduced. His dependence on a particular job was attenuated. The expansion of the concept of productivity diminished his perception of the importance of factory work. This tended to increase his awareness of a lack of relationship between his repetitive job and the final product. As a consequence, his sense of identity was diminished and his alienation increased.

It is with respect to developmental changes of this kind that generational gaps probably are widest. The older worker tends to retain his sense of the importance of productive work and therefore is able to take pride in it. Many younger workers, who grew up in the new milieu—at least prior to the recent recession—do not understand such attitudes. Nor does the older worker understand the newer attitudes or the social or productive styles that respond to them.

Contemporary problems may be at least as difficult to cope with as those that arose from poverty. Crises of self-esteem arising from relative abundance and the availability of social welfare may cut deeply into definitions of identity. Increased use of machines in sophisticated processes may cause many individuals, although fewer among the highly skilled or the unimaginative, to regard themselves as supernumeraries or even to become confused with respect to the distinction between the human and non-human—a consequence that could have a profoundly evil influence upon politics and upon social and productive styles.

This issue raises the question of a possible inherent incompatibility between productive achievement and the sense of accomplishment. If the latter is important to the sense of identity, as I suspect it is, material security may erode satisfaction in life, thus producing pathologies of behavior: apathy and a deadening of sensibility in some and a disordered search for thrills or a mission in life in others.

Whether we can control the exigencies of nature and at the same time confront man with creative tasks essential to his sense of productivity is a poignant issue for politics. Perhaps we need not worry, for the pollution problem and the energy problem do not seem to indicate an absence of challenge. Yet their seeming inaccessibility to intervention by any agency other than mammoth and impersonal governments is not entirely reassuring. And they may foster style changes in productivity and in society that are pathological.

The Individual and Social Costs

With changed attitudes toward work, it should not be surprising that there is a receptivity toward new life styles better adapted to these new attitudes. On the other hand, it does not follow that the new attitudes are genuinely functional. Large and unnecessary social costs are involved in sloppy manufacture and repair work.

We all recognize these problems in general terms. We deplore them when we suffer from them. However, on the whole, we fail to see the relationships between our attitudes and our life styles and their consequences. The interrelationships are too remote, too indirect, and too ambiguous. In the same way, individual acts of industrial sabotage seem relatively costless. And, indeed, they would be relatively costless if the individual engaging in them were the only one who did so. However, the attitudes that motivate him motivate many others just like him, and the resulting social cost is very high.

This illustrative example does not prove that each relative success with respect to some of the problems facing society generates new problems, new discontents, and new identity crises, although each change in the environment does change the perception of social relationships and social meaning. Yet, it surely suggests one or more of these consequences. Only the most original and perceptive minds of each generation will be capable of forecasting the ways in which social, economic, and political change will affect the future and the

perceptions human beings will have of the meaningful character of their roles. It is hardly likely that they will be sufficiently influential to alert the mass of the population to these
remote consequences, particularly if the present costs of
avoiding them are clear and substantial.

Imagine the response if during the Great Depression of the
1930s some misguided genius had attempted to alert the
nation to the perils of pollution under conditions of a future
prosperity the individuals of that time would not have
thought possible, and if he had suggested a modest tax
scheme—or, alternatively, an increase in the cost of production—to protect against those perils. If any notice would have
been taken of him at all, it likely would have been as a source
of laughter or as a butt of anger. Moreover, this response,
although not entirely appropriate, would have been not entirely inappropriate either. It was more important to deal
with the problem of prosperity first, which we did not then
know how to solve, than it was to anticipate the problems of
pollution if the problem of prosperity were solved.

In the best of all possible worlds, some resources will be
made available to explore the parameters of problems that
can be anticipated by intelligent men. In a world in which
resources are scarce, the mechanisms that guard against a
diversion of resources to the study of hypothetical future
problems are eufunctional. Even in prosperous worlds, resources are not unlimited. Thus, in present-day society, in
which the ecological problem has become severe, there are
serious questions as to who shall bear the costs of control and
how they shall be borne. Each suggested solution sacrifices
some alternative gain. Each principle of spreading the costs
conflicts with some alternative principle and thereby conflicts with someone's sense of justice. Each putative solution
will have differential impact on some human beings' perceptions of their identity or on the authenticity of their expressions of their being.

Despite the prior comments, it may be possible to acquire
better insight into how social change affects perception and

style of behavior. We know that our anticipations of the future will sometimes fail, that problems will always exist, that solutions will always impact differentially, that perceptions will always be altered, and that some senses of identity and some expressions of authenticity will always be injured. The certainty of such changes, however, does not mean that we cannot attempt to minimize damage, to facilitate authenticity, and to preserve the sense of identity.

Style Exaggeration and Its Consequences

We do not know enough about the social process to know whether damage from style exaggeration can be minimized in all cases. For instance, consider the political role in contemporary society. Some have suggested that the demands of the highest political offices, for instance, the presidency, are so great that only very abnormal individuals seek them. Yet, clearly we need people to fill these offices.

In some cases, where society greatly needs a role to be filled, the rewards attached to it may facilitate the development in those individuals initially predisposed toward it of those very motivations that are dysfunctional in excess. Thus, at least under current conditions, society may require roles that—although highly rewarded and serving as a source of a sense of identity—impede authenticity.

Perhaps a slight clue to a possible solution to this problem can be discovered by examining the possibility that the rewards offered by society may emphasize in political personalities those dysfunctional tendencies that make them successful in the role. In the first place, it is not clear that the success of political leaders in performing societal and political functions stems from an excess of competitiveness, although in an imperfect world some of it may be necessary for role performance. It instead may be the case that it is success in achieving the role, rather than success in performing it, that may require an excess in competitiveness.

If the latter hypothesis is correct, then a society that manifests prominent particular styles of behavior may encourage these styles in politically prone persons so much that they become dysfunctional for the society. In a heroic age, political leaders may romantically risk more than prudence would dictate. In a bourgeois age, political leaders may engage in excesses of deceit and calculation. In a scientific age, political leaders may too easily accept the technologies produced by science without considering the political and moral consequences of their employment.

In those cases in which a society manifests a style as strongly as this, it may be said to lack moderation. It may also inhibit authenticity, for each style represents an exaggeration of some aspect of being. This does not occur in any simple fashion, however. Some expressions of heroism are responsive to passion; others are responsive to idealism or the sacred. In the first case, they may be viewed as an expression of manliness; in the latter case, as an expression of a quest for sanctity. The bourgeois calculating style appeals to certain aspects of mind and exaggerates those tendencies in it. Heroism exaggerates a sacrifice of the self to the community or to spirit. The bourgeois spirit exaggerates the self and atomizes it. Puritanism exaggerates compulsive dysfunctions. Estheticism exaggerates hysterical dysfunctions.

Society and Authenticity

Exaggerated tendencies in style stem from different aspects of being. These different aspects of being cannot be homogenized. However, a society of sufficient complexity probably can provide roles that permit the manifestation of each of the tendencies. And, if this complex society is sufficiently permeable, individuals then can be encouraged to engage in a diversity of activities that manifest these often conflicting tendencies. Conceivably, if such variety does not confuse the individual, it might serve to maintain a viable level of authenticity, in which each of the aspects of being will find some substantial manifestation in behavior and serve as a constraint on excess.

A society with this type of complexity would not eliminate the potential for alienation—or even its occurrence to some extent—and it would not eliminate problems. However, it might reduce those exaggerations that generate unnecessary problems. A political leader who has been exposed to and constrained by such a variety of activities might be protected against the tendency of the chase for the office and the exercise of the powers of the office to exaggerate in him those abnormal characteristics that may have predisposed him to seek it in the first place.

I do not suggest that such a complex society would eliminate the cyclical nature of esthetic expression or developmental changes in style in society at large. Esthetic cycles probably follow an at least partly semiautonomous pattern and social style is related to the problems generated by the complexly interrelated natural, social, cultural, and economic environments. Perhaps, however, sharp alternations of the pattern can be moderated, or at least offset, by countervailing influences. Whatever may or may not be true of some specialized social roles, where perhaps unbalanced or even impoverished personalities are required, perhaps we can at least avoid that extreme situation in which the bulk of the elite, or even of the population at large, is desensitized to essential aspects of being, whether these be sensual, intellectual, or spiritual.

Society and Identity

In addition to protecting influences and life styles related to the various aspects of being, thus facilitating authenticity, we require social, economic, and political arrangements that maintain the identities of the citizens. This may involve relative equality with respect to a number of things: the vote, the right to education, the meeting of at least minimal medical needs, the assurance of meaningful work and meaningful recreational opportunities, and the assurance of meaningful (and not demeaning) assistance in case of adversity or accident. A human society will also permit equal opportunity to individuals to pursue those inequalities that respond to existential differences in their being and that do not demean or subject other people: in creations of the mind, in exercises of bodily skill, in developing productive techniques, or in the capacity to earn those of the goods of life that are needed to satisfy tastes, special abilities, or ambitions.

Society and Taste

A human society is one in which individuals exercise taste and sensibility. In discussing creativity, one of the distinctions I made between the conscious and the preconscious mind involved the capacity of the preconscious mind to scan for and to recognize "fits" among phenomena. The same capacity is made manifest when we recognize a particular individual. If the individual has a prominent characteristic, we can explain that we recognized him by means of that characteristic. Usually, however, our ability to articulate how recognition occurs is inadequate for teaching others how to recognize what we recognize: consider in this respect, for instance, the art of the tea taster.

For similar reasons, we usually cannot articulate those fine distinctions in social or moral situations that are necessary to account for our behavior. Much important social and moral behavior cannot be compressed within the framework of explicit rules. Thus, the concept of taste adds to our conception of transfinitely stable identity.

Taste and sensitivity—the ability to resonate finely to situations and to people—are required for appropriate social behavior. Some lack this capability because their behavior is derived from, rather than merely constrained by, a set of rules. Others interpret the behavior of people in terms of stereotypes or of their own needs. This impoverishment of perception diminishes their humanity and threatens their sense of identity.

Sensitivity to the needs of others is a necessary, but not a sufficient, condition for taste or sensibility. The sociopath is sensitive to the requirements of others. He could not manipulate them so easily were this not true. However, he lacks taste or sensibility, for he would not manipulate them if he understood the inappropriateness of manipulation or if he had a firm sense of identity. Thus, sensitivity involves openness to information whereas taste involves the sense of appropriateness in responding.

In some ways the sociopath is a bad example, for he lacks a comprehension of the existence of a moral order. Lack of taste could be even more clearly recognized in the case of those individuals who recognize the existence of a moral order, who wish to observe it, but who are incapable of making appropriate distinctions that are not directly reducible to rules. Thus, for instance, at the Democratic Convention in 1968 the demonstration after the showing of the Kennedy movie was contrary to the rules. The chairman was within his rights in attempting to stop the demonstration. However, his action lacked taste. In the first place, it would have been appropriate to show some respect for so widespread a sentiment even if one disagreed with it and even if it was technically contrary to the rules. In the second place, the showing of respect under these conditions would have had a beneficial influence upon the political process. The chairman's action was neither wrong nor ill intentioned, but it did lack taste.

Although taste can be dangerous if it becomes overly refined, as in the sensibility of the decadents, a balanced capacity for taste is essential to a human society. Civility, which requires taste, is a requirement for human politics. If one were engaged on a mission to undermine the foundations upon which a human society might be built, he would have no stronger weapon in his arsenal than that of incivility.

Society and Alienation

A human society is one in which alienation is accepted as a natural potentiality. It is only when one understands the ineradicable and ineluctable character of otherness that one is willing to concede autonomy, and hence potential alienation, to others. Only such a willingness will produce that recognition of sufficient identity of interest between the self and others to solve particular problems. Those who will not accept this necessary potential for alienation will be driven to compel others to conform to the dictates of their own reason and needs. Anyone who resists, anything that defies understanding, anything that manifests an unexpected development thereby reveals itself as alien and invites destruction.

Society can be restructured to improve the sense of identity, and to facilitate authenticity, to encourage productivity, and to generate creativity if alienation is recognized as ineluctably potential in life. If we recognize that problems will always occur, that conflict will always exist, that resources are always limited, that every improvement in something involves differential costs for some people, that harmony and mutuality of interest can apply only to selected aspects and not to the whole of existence, we can better perceive those acts of reconstruction that can move us toward a human society.

Whether we can achieve a human society is a question this book cannot answer. Our procedure has been analytical and hypothetical. Whether the conflicting design requirements for a human society in which authentic men participate can be met depends upon the capacity of the world of the future to accommodate sufficiently the conflicting demands of personality and social organizations. It depends also upon the ability of men to perceive solutions and to possess the desire and the social and material means for acting upon their perceptions.

There is an ultimate particularity that defies all our generalizations. We must continually return to the open world of experience to refresh our concepts, our ideas, our generalizations, and our theories. It is the union of the particular with the general that generates meaning and governs understanding. Except by accident, a human society will be built only by those who recognize this. Man's feet are in the mud and his eyes look to the stars.

Appendix

Mao's Theory of Economic Stages and of Value

Since completion of the manuscript of this book, more information has become available concerning Mao Tse-tung's position on Marxian theory, particularly with respect to his criticisms of the political economy of the Soviet Union. Although I shall use this material cautiously, as my information is based upon a secondary source,[1] even this degree of information may shed valuable light on an important variation of the Communist theory of alienation because of the close relationship of its sociological aspect to the Marxian theory of value.

One of the first things a reader notes is Mao's use of the concept of stages. The idea of stages is not new with Mao, for it is present in Engels's *Origins of the Family,* in the anthropological writings of Lewis Morgan, to whom Engels was indebted, and in Marx's economic writings, although not in the unilinear form often attributed to him, as those familiar with Marx's writings on Asia are aware.

However, Mao distinguishes the measures appropriate to different stages of society far more explicitly than did Stalin.

For instance, Mao's distinction between collective owner-ship and ownership by all permits him to refer to "steal-ing" or improper requisition of the property of individ-uals or teams or brigades by higher levels in socialism.

The reader of my book *Justice, Human Nature, and Political Obligation* will see the relationship between Mao's belief that rules of behavior should be related to societal conditions and my claim, in contradistinction to the position of John Rawls, that systems of value simi-larly ought to be related.

Mao's distinctions concerning stages are related to his position on contradictions. Mao sees each stage of society as containing contradictions, but he distinguishes between those contradictions that require a "big revolution" that entails civil war and those that require only smaller revolutions that do not entail civil war.

Although Mao attempts to relate his theory to Marx's theory of revolution, he extends Lenin's (Trotsky's?) "weak link" theory by arguing that the less-developed areas are the weakest links in the world capitalist system because the superstructure is the least developed in them. Unlike Althu-ser's use of the "weak link" explanation, Mao's use has substantive content. However, precisely because of this, it constitutes a fundamental reformulation, if not a con-tradiction, of Marxian theory rather than a deduction from it—a distinction that, as we will see, Mao attempts to finesse.

Mao runs into trouble when he attempts to determine the criteria by means of which the transition between stages is related to environmental conditions. For instance, according to Levy, Mao states that a " 'decisive condition' for the transition from team to commune ownership is that the economic income of the commune must be greater than one half of the gross income. . . ."

Levy argues that this is not a totally satisfactory criterion because ownership, and therefore income, can easily be manipulated by administrative fiat. Levy's criticism is relevant only on the mistaken assumption that a theory is expected to predict in the absence of feedback between variables, for example, between administrative decisions and the conditions that permit major social change. The real problem in Mao's formulation lies rather in the apparent belief of Mao, in common with other Marxian theorists, that the conditions "calling for" a transition in stages ought to be deduced from a supratheory applying to all the variables of real history rather than to the selected variables of a particular theory. And Mao's eclectic use of "conditions" is major evidence that he does not possess such a supratheory.

I argued earlier in this book that, in principle, there can be no such supratheory. Mao attempts to finesse this problem through a distinction between pure and applied Marxism, but at the price of destroying an articulated relationship between the pure and the applied theory. Mao's theory of stages is divorced from a self-generated progression in the forces of production and instead is generated by decisions in the super-structure. Therefore he cannot explain why the alternatives in social relations are those foreseen by Marx. Except for his acceptance of the concept of surplus value, and its accompanying concept of exploitation, he has no justification for his preference for Communism or for his distinctions between types of economic systems. And, as I have earlier shown, the concept of surplus value is indefensible. Mao's preference for Communism is existentially voluntaristic rather than "scientific" as Marx uses the term or as I use it to account for ethical decisions.

A systems orientation, on the other hand, would produce two sets of questions: first, "What are the conditions under which an existing system can maintain itself or be prevented from maintaining itself?" and, second, "What are the conditions under which a new form of organization of society or the economy can be maintained?" This is not very different from asking under what conditions a species can maintain itself and under what conditions an evolutionary adaptation might be sustained.

It is likely that Levy's interpretation of Mao's position is correct. Had Mao approached the question from a systems standpoint, it would remain an open empirical question whether a transition is desirable or, even if it is, which of alternative forms of institutionalization is preferable. Thus, the fact that a change in conditions predisposes toward an evolutionary adaptation does not mean that a species would or should prefer it. If, for instance, industrialization were to change the environment in such ways that certain types of biological and social "mutations," for instance, Communism, are highly probable it would not mean that these are to be preferred. Indeed, if foreseen and properly understood, wise men might attempt to prevent them and to facilitate a more desirable, or at least less bad, alternative.

Another serious problem in Mao's thought is the distinction between collective ownership and ownership by the whole people. Although in principle one can distinguish between policies that promote the common good and those that do not, the concept of ownership by the whole people applies a term that has no meaning in use and that obscures those "power" relationships that determine or influence the use of goods or of the "forces of production."

Mao does recognize the possibilities of conflict even in Communist society; and he is aware, as are the Rumanians, that power relationships may be "misused" if, in Chinese Communist terms, a "bourgeois" mentality persists. However, once he divorces ideology and power relationships from their material foundations in social forces and social relations—as they are specified in the standard Communist definitions of class structure that are so dependent on legal ownership—the intellectual rationale for his terminology and his program collapses. Yet the revisions in standard Communist formulations that Mao makes are necessitated by defects in the definitions of "forces" and "relations" of production upon which they are based: defects that experience has made apparent to all. If, in addition, one dispenses with the concept of "surplus" value, as we have shown to be necessary, both the inchoate ethical presumptions that justify, and the materialistic presumptions that predict, Communist revolutions lose whatever slight respectability might have survived the prior critique.

Mao attempts to avoid this conclusion through his reliance upon the superstructure as the motor of revolution. But "superstructures" cannot be divorced from concrete social relations, even if there is no one-to-one relationship between them. If we recognize this, the problems of how to organize and manage the economy, and to relate it to other social institutions, reemerges as a fresh problem requiring fresh analysis and fresh conclusions. The failure adequately to recognize this is the Achilles heel of Marx's treatment of the concept of alienation. It constitutes a reactionary element in Marx's valiant attempt to free social thought from the "bourgeois" abstractions that characterized it in the time in which he lived and wrote.

Notes

Chapter 1. Origins of the Problem

1. Louis Althuser, *For Marx* (London: Allen Lane, The Penguin Press, 1969, pp. 66-67.

2. Ibid., p. 76.

3. Ibid., p. 95.

4. Ibid., pp. 95-96.

5. Ibid., p. 97.

6. Ibid., p. 111.

7. Ibid.

8. Donald J. Munro, "The Chinese View of Alienation," *China Quarterly*, no. 59 (July/September 1974), pp. 580-82.

9. Althuser, *For Marx*, p. 242.

10. Jürgen Habermas, *Theory and Practice* (Boston: Beacon Press, 1973, 1973), p. 195.

11. Ibid., p. 196.

12. Ibid., p. 3.

13. Ibid., p. 7.

14. Ibid., pp. 7-8.

15. Ibid., p. 8.
16. Ibid., p. 9.
17. Ibid., p. 11.
18. Ibid., p. 17.
19. Ibid.
20. Ibid.
21. Ibid., p. 18.
22. Ibid., p. 32.

Chapter 2. Resolution of the Epistemological Problem

1. See Morton A. Kaplan, *System and Process in International Politics* (New York: John Wiley & Sons, 1957), pp. 271-80; reprinted in Morton A. Kaplan, *Macropolitics: Essays on the Philosophy and Science of Politics* (Chicago: Aldine Publishing Co., 1969), pp. 156-57. The only similar position I have come across is in Alan Gewirth, "The Normative Structure of Action," *Review of Metaphysics* 30, 2 (December 1971): 238-61.

2. Kaplan, *Macropolitics*, pp. 42-43.

3. Morton A. Kaplan, *On Freedom and Human Dignity: The Importance of the Sacred in Politics* (Morristown, N.J.: General Learning Press, 1973), pp. 34-35.

4. J. M. Burgers, "Causality and Anticipation," *Science* 189 (18 July 1975): 194-98.

Appendix. Mao's Theory of Economic Stages and of Value

1. See Richard Levy, "New Light on Mao: 2. His Views on the Soviet Union's Political Economy," *China Quarterly*, no. 61 (March 1975), pp. 95-117, which is based upon *Mao Tse-tung ssu-hsiang wan sui*, 2 vols.

Index

205